# INSIGHT GUIDES

# BARCELONA
## smart guide

Discovery
CHANNEL

APA PUBLICATIONS L
Part of the Langenscheidt Publishing Group

# Contents

## Areas

## A–Z

**Left:** a building in the Ribera district of Barcelona.

**Left:** Parc Diagonal Mar.

**Left:** taking a stroll in
Sant Pere.

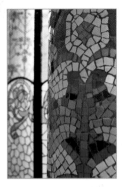

# Barcelona

Unlike most other great cities, Barcelona has no well-trodden tourist itinerary forming the reason to visit, but rather its organic whole forms the main attraction. Its cohesive visual charm has made it the first city to win the RIBA gold medal for architecture, celebrating the shady medieval streets as much as the kaleidoscopic Modernista creations and futuristic urban sculpture.

## Barcelona Facts and Figures

Area: 100 sq km (39 sq miles)
Population density: 15,779 inhabitants per sq km
Visitors staying overnight in central Barcelona: 14 million per year
No. of World Heritage Sites: 9 (7 buildings by Antoni Gaudí and 2 by Lluís Domènech i Montaner)
No. of museums: 65
No. of parks and gardens: 67
No. of cinema screens: 205
No. of bar terraces: 3,073
Most visited sites: Sagrada Família (2.5m), CosmoCaixa (1.8m), Museu FC Barcelona (1.3m)

## Geography

Despite its efficient public transport system, most visitors will walk almost everywhere in Barcelona. With a dense population, and any real urban sprawl prevented by mountains, rivers and sea, the city is incredibly compact, and only a handful of sights – such as Park Güell, Montjuïc and the Sagrada Família – are more than an easy stroll from the centre.

As maps are invariably oriented with north-west at the top instead of north, *barcelonins* have devised their own way of giving directions, particularly in the grid-like Eixample, to avoid confusion. '*Mar*' and '*muntanya*' ('sea' and 'mountain') are used instead of 'north' and 'south', while 'Besòs' and 'Llobregat' refer to the rivers running to the right and left of most maps and are used instead of 'east' and 'west'.

## Population

Soaring property prices and a high rate of immigration have placed a lot of pressure on the city's residents, and there are frequent demonstrations against property speculation and the difficulties faced by first-time buyers. Increasingly the Old City is inhabited by foreigners, who tend to be more enamoured with the district's ancient and leaky flats than the Catalans, who – given the choice – prefer more modern accommodation. Down-to-earth, local *barrios* include Poble Sec and Gràcia, while the uptown zones (Sarrià, Pedralbes and so on) are the domain of the moneyed classes.

## Climate

Winter days rarely dip below 5°C (41°F), and July normally sees top temperatures of around 32°C (90°F). While Barcelona enjoys a relatively moderate climate compared to the highs and lows of, say, Madrid, it can

**Right:** historic Plaça Fossar de les Moreres in the Born.

get very humid in summer, and visitors should plan their days accordingly, with plenty of pit stops and not too much walking. As ever, spring and autumn are optimum times to visit, but January often surprises with a month of blue skies and mild temperatures. Most rainfall occurs around May and, particularly, September and October, but is usually restricted to short, heavy showers.

## Festivals

Catalans are famous for their *'seny'*, an elusive word combining elements of nous, sobriety and good sense, but much is also made of their occasional *'rauxa'*, the counterpoint to this. Implying a slight craziness and capacity for wild partying, it's given full vent in the panoply of the city's fiestas.

Given the absence of extreme climatic conditions, what's on at any given time could be a more important factor in planning a trip. The no-holds-barred blowout festival of La Mercè in September is the queen of them all, but at most times of year there is some sort of public celebration going on. There are music festivals ranging from jazz to techno, sporting events, film, documentary, video and art festivals, along with all-night neighbourhood parties that celebrate nothing other than community.

SEE ALSO FESTIVALS, P.48–51

# Highlights

▲ **Palau de la Música Catalana** Domènech i Montaner's concert hall is one of the most florid expressions of Modernisme. ▶ **Museu Picasso** A unique collection of the artist's early work, most of it from his years spent in the city.

▶ **MNAC** A huge display of Catalan artistic endeavour, from Romanesque murals and Gothic paintings to Modernista furniture.

▲ **Fundació Joan Miró** Bold and colourful works by arguably the region's greatest artist, housed in building worth the visit alone.

▲ **The beaches** Seven uninterrupted kilometres of golden sand. ▶ **Antoni Gaudí's Barcelona** The Sagrada Família, La Pedrera and the Casa Batlló are just some of the architect's masterpieces.

# Plaça de Catalunya and La Rambla

The Plaça de Catalunya is not a grand, arcaded square in the traditional Spanish style, but is nonetheless a pivotal hub in terms of transport. For most tourists, however, this is the portal to La Rambla, one of the most famous boulevards in Europe, and for many people one of the distinguishing features of Barcelona. Despite the huge numbers of tourists that surge along it and the somewhat tacky souvenir shops that line it, it never fails to entertain.

See Atlas Pages 138–139

### Plaça de Catalunya ①

Once this was the geographical centre of Barcelona, before urban sprawl altered the shape of the city – if you look in the middle of the square itself you will find paving stones arranged into the shape of a star, which, they say, marked the centre of the capital of Catalonia.

### Rambla de Canaletes

Between the top of La Rambla and the Columbus monument where it ends there are five different parts to the promenade. The first, Rambla de Canaletes, is named after the **Font de Canaletes** ②, one of the symbols of Barcelona. It is a favourite meeting place, and posses of retired men regularly gather here to put the world to rights.

### Rambla dels Estudis

Next is the Rambla dels Estudis, so named because the 16th-century university was here.

The **Reial Acadèmia de Ciències i Arts** on the right also houses the **Teatre Poliorama**, which has regular performances. On its exterior is the clock that has been the official timekeeper of the city since 1891. Further along (beyond the former Philippine

Tobacco Factory, now a hotel, *see p.64*) is the baroque **Betlem** ③ church, a long and rather depressing bulk. Opposite is the **Palau Moja** (also known as the Palau Marquès de Comillas), an important 18th-century classical building.

### Rambla de les Flors

Next is the Rambla de Sant Josep, better known as the Rambla de les Flors for the

At the end of La Rambla the **Monument a Colom**, an 80m- (262ft-) tall column topped with a statue of Christopher Columbus, gives panoramic views from the top, reached by a small lift. It's open daily 9am–8.30pm in summer and 10am–6pm in winter.

**Left:** a 'human statue' entertains the crowd on La Rambla.

(opera house) and has a grander air. Opposite is the legendary **Cafè de l'Òpera**, going since 1929 and which still retains much of its charm. The other terraces that line La Rambla along this stretch are largely spurned by locals, but as long as you do not expect the ultimate culinary experience it is tempting to sip a cool drink and watch the world go by.
SEE ALSO BARS AND CAFÉS, P.28; MUSIC, P.92

### Rambla de Santa Mònica

The promenade opens up again into the **Plaça del Teatre**, where, in the 16th century, the city's first theatre was built. The square marks the beginning of the Rambla de Santa Mònica, the last stretch of La Rambla before it reaches the harbour. This stretch was once the most elegant and home to the crème of Catalan society, then fell into disrepute and abandonment. It has been cleaned up in recent years, but the prostitution is still all too evident. The Rambla Santa Mònica is lined with caricaturists, portrait painters and artisans, and a craft market is held here at the weekend.

flower stalls that have stood here since the 19th century. On the right is the **Palau de la Virreina** ④, a magnificent 18th-century rococo building, which nowadays houses an information centre for all things cultural, a ticket office and two exhibition spaces coming off its handsome courtyard. A little further along is the entrance to the city's best-loved market, the **Mercat de la Boqueria** ⑤, or Mercat de Sant Josep.

La Rambla then widens slightly, and becomes the **Pla de la Boqueria**, distinguished by the recently restored Joan Miró mosaic, dating back to the 1970s. This spot once had more sinister overtones: it was where the bodies of executed men would hang to deter would-be criminals in the 14th century. On the corner is the **Casa Bruno Quadras**, built by Josep Vilaseca in 1891. The extravagant oriental dec-

A small brass plaque at the foot of the 19th-century cast-iron **Font de Canaletes** carries the legend that all those who drink its waters will always return to Barcelona. The fountain is at its most jubilant when Barça football fans of all ages gather there to celebrate yet another victory.

oration includes umbrellas, fans and a great Chinese dragon.
SEE ALSO MARKETS, P.78

### Rambla dels Caputxins

At this point the Rambla dels Caputxins begins, so called because, until 1775, the left side was the site of the Capuchin Convent. This stretch is dominated by the **Gran Teatre del Liceu** ⑥

**Right:** Joan Miró mosaic on the Pla de la Boqueria.
**Above left:** the entrance to the Mercat de la Boqueria.

# Barri Gòtic

The Gothic Quarter, or Barri Gòtic, is a dense web of historic buildings and shady atmospheric squares nestled between La Rambla and the Via Laietana, and has formed the central part of the Old City since Roman times. Layer upon layer of different architectural styles illustrate the different periods of Barcelona's history, from remnants of the Roman city to contemporary architectural solutions seen in renovation work and extensions to old buildings. Gothic predominates, however, reflecting the glorious medieval period when Catalonia was at its height.

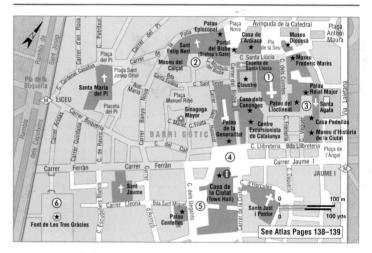

See Atlas Pages 138–139

## Catedral ①

The area is dominated by the immense cathedral, built mostly in medieval times, with its elaborate neo-Gothic façade added in the 20th century. Its main entrance overlooks the **Avinguda de la Catedral**, a wide-open space spreading out at the foot of the steps. An antiques market takes place here on Thursdays, and at the weekend the gatherings of *sardana* dancers form large bouncing circles. Next to the cathedral is the **chapel** dedicated to Santa Llúcia and, in front of it, the 15th-century

**Casa de l'Ardiaca** (Archdeacon's House). The sculpted letters in front, by Catalan artist Joan Brossa, spell out 'Barcino', the Roman name for the city.

SEE ALSO CHURCHES, P.38

## Roman Gates

Beyond that is one of the main Roman gates to the Old City, the **Portal del Bisbe** (Bishop's Gate). The towers date from the 1st century BC, but the name came later, from the nearby 18th-century Bishop's Palace. Alongside the Portal is the **Palau Episcopal**, built in 1769

around a 12th-century courtyard, which is the only remaining evidence of the original palace after centuries of modifications.

## Plaça Sant Felip Neri ②

From here, Montjuïc del Bisbe leads into Plaça Sant

Both the **Casa de la Ciutat** and the **Palau de la Generalitat** can be visited on certain public holidays, such as La Mercè in September. During Sant Jordi (23 April) the Generalitat is at its most spectacular, its elegant patio filled with red roses.

Barcelona. A dramatic statue of the Virgin and Child stands on the top of the church, creating a distinctive element in the skyline. The square is at its most festive on 24 September, the day of La Mercè, when the city's giants and human castles greet the dignitaries coming out of Mass, before the real *festa major* of Barcelona takes off.
SEE ALSO FESTIVALS, P.51

### ⑥ Plaça Reial

The infamous Plaça Reial is another Barcelona landmark and one of the most handsome yet decadent of its squares. Attempts to 'clean it up' have done little to change its character, so tourists still jostle with junkies, and backpackers share benches with tramps. Restaurants, bars and clubs predominate, like the well-established **Jamboree** jazz club, or Sidecar, with DJs and live music.

On Sunday, stamp and coin collectors gather around the **Font de Les Tres Gràcies** and the two lampposts designed by Antoni Gaudí. Its uniform, arcaded buildings were constructed by Francesc Daniel Molina on the plot where the Capuchin Convent once stood.
SEE ALSO MUSIC, P.93

Felip Neri. This small square is a treasure, enclosed by heavy stone buildings and happily neglected, which increases its historic impact. The pockmarked façade of the 18th-century church of **Sant Felip Neri** is a melancholy reminder that a large number of children were killed here when a bomb dropped nearby during the Civil War.

### Plaça del Rei ③

The Plaça del Rei, a fine medieval square, lies between the cathedral and the northern Roman wall and was once the courtyard of the royal palace. At one end is the **Palau Reial Major**, with vast vaulted ceilings and 14th-century rose windows. On the right is a 16th-century Gothic mansion, **Casa Padellàs**, which serves as the entrance to the **Museu d'Història de la Ciutat**. The sculpture is by the Basque artist Eduardo Chillida.
SEE ALSO MUSEUMS AND GALLERIES, P.85

### Plaça Sant Jaume ④

The area that today forms the Plaça Sant Jaume was inaugurated in 1823, after the church of Sant Jaume that once stood here burnt down. The scene of many a demonstration in bad times and many a celebration in good times, it forms the civic heart of the city, with the neoclassical façade of the **Casa de la Ciutat** (Town Hall) facing that of the **Palau de la Generalitat**, home to the Catalan government.

### Plaça de la Mercè ⑤

Down towards the waterfront is a less grandiose but equally significant square, dominated by the 18th-century church of **La Mercè**, one of the patron saints of

# Sant Pere and Born

Now Barcelona's most fashionable neighbourhood, the Born was not always so lucky, and took a battering in the 18th century, when half of it was destroyed to make way for Felipe V's hated citadel. Nowadays the citadel has gone, and the wonderful Parc de la Ciutadella stands in its place, while the medieval streets of the area are home to the coolest boutiques and funkiest bars in the city. Sitting to the north east of Via Laietana, the Born is usually used to describe the area below Carrer de la Princesa, and Sant Pere is used for the neighbourhood above it, but you will often hear 'La Ribera' used to describe the whole neighbourhood.

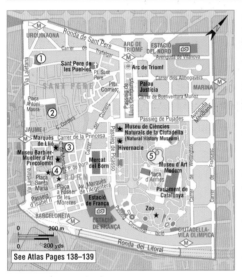

See Atlas Pages 138–139

lampposts on Passeig de Gràcia.
SEE ALSO MODERNISME, P.80; MUSIC, P.92

## Mercat de Santa Caterina ②

Also in this neighbourhood is the colourful, undulating Mercat de Santa Caterina, designed by the late Enric Miralles, the Catalan architect behind the Scottish Parliament. This bustling indoor food market is a focal point of the area, as much frequented by chatting neighbours sipping coffee as shoppers. At the rear of the building you can see medieval and Roman remains under glass.
SEE ALSO MARKETS, P.79

## Carrer de Montcada

To the other side of Carrer de la Princesa is the Old City's best-known street, Carrer de Montcada. It is lined with the medieval mansions of the wealthy merchants who used to live in this area. Montcada has become museum street supreme since the 1960s, but it is a lot more besides and can be enjoyed on many levels. As you jostle with the crowds in the narrow street, glance up at the gargoyles and elegant medieval arches on top-floor terraces.

## Palau de la Música Catalana ①

The slightly scruffy neighbourhood of Sant Pere is largely ignored by tourists, but boasts a couple of architectural jewels. The first is the **Palau de la Música**

Between the two entrances to the park on Passeig Picasso is a large modern sculpture in a transparent cube. This is *Homage to Picasso*, by leading Catalan artist Antoni Tàpies.

**Catalana**, a concert hall and masterpiece of Modernista design, created by architect Domènech i Montaner in 1908. At the other end of the same street lies the much-renovated 10th-century church **Sant Pere de les Puel·les**, a former Benedictine monastery. It sits in the comparative tranquillity of triangular Plaça Sant Pere, looking over the delicate Modernista drinking fountain designed by Pere Falqués, famed for his benches-cum-

**Left:** the Modernista Palau de la Música Catalana.

**Mar** ④. This splendid work of Catalan Gothic is considered by many – and justly so – to be the most beautiful church in Barcelona. Its soaring majesty is uplifting, and should not be missed. In front is the **Plaça Santa Maria**, once the church's graveyard. Its Gothic fountain is one of the oldest in the city, dating from 1402.
SEE ALSO CHURCHES, P.38–9

### Parc de la Ciutadella ⑤

Once upon a time the Parc de la Ciutadella was the city's only park, and it is still its most visited. The name, La Ciutadella, has its origins in the citadel which Felipe V had built on this land to control the people of Barcelona after their rebellion during the War of Spanish Succession. It is a verdant, peaceful place to stroll, with a boating lake and various sculptures and buildings of interest. It houses the **Museu de Ciències Naturals de la Ciutadella** (Natural History Museum), the **Zoo** and the beautiful **Hivernacle**, an elegant greenhouse bursting with tropical plants.
SEE ALSO CHILDREN, P.37;
MUSEUMS AND GALLERIES, P.86;
PARKS, GARDENS AND
BEACHES, P.100–101

The **Plaça Fossar de les Moreres** is a memorial to the fallen in the 1714 siege of Barcelona, who are buried here in the former cemetery. Restored in 1986 by Carme Fiol, who added the controversial 'Eternal Flame', it is a favourite venue for Catalan nationalists to meet on 11 September, **La Diada Nacional**, the day the siege ended, and the Catalan national holiday *(see p.51)*.

The **Museu Picasso** ③ opened in 1963 and now occupies five mansions: Palau Berenguer d'Aguilar, Baró de Castellet, Meca, Casa Mauri and Finestres. Opposite is the another noble Gothic palace, the **Marquès de Lló**, which until recently housed the Museu Tèxtil and has retained its lively café in the courtyard. Adjoining it is the Palau Nadal,

housing the **Museu Barbier-Mueller d'Art Precolombí**, a museum of pre-Columbian art.
SEE ALSO MUSEUMS AND
GALLERIES, P.85–6

### Santa Maria del Mar

This street runs to the wide pedestrian boulevard and former jousting ground, the **Passeig del Born**, with the old Born market, a handsome structure of slatted iron, at the far end. To the right is the church of **Santa Maria del**

**Right:** trendy bars abound in this area.

# Raval

Walking down La Rambla from Plaça de Catalunya, the section of the Old City to the right-hand side is known as the Raval. In the 1930s this area was one of the most densely populated urban areas in the world, when it became derogatively known as the Barri Xino (Chinese Quarter). It is still given a wide berth by many of Barcelona's inhabitants. However, it is one of the districts of the city with the most potential, and a stimulating area in which to wander and observe. Although some areas are still run-down and at times edgy, some of the most interesting cultural activities in the city are now taking place here.

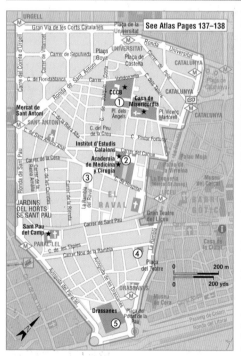

## Plaça Vicenç Martorell

The upper part of the Raval has long been thought of as more salubrious, and here you will find young couples sitting in the arcaded Plaça Vicenç Martorell drinking coffee while their children run around the playground in the centre. The large, handsome building dominating the square is a former convent dating from 1635, now used as district council offices. Behind the newspaper kiosk, the long-neglected **Casa de la Misericòrdia** (1583), formerly a hospice for aban-

doned children, has been cleverly restored, complete with interior palm tree, to make more council offices.

## Casa de la Caritat

Nearby is the **Plaça dels Àngels**, which opens up into the unexpected space dominated by Richard Meier's breathtaking **MACBA** ① (Museu d'Art Contemporani de Barcelona). The museum was built in the grounds of the enormous 18th-century Casa de la Caritat (poorhouse). The former hospice has been transformed into the **CCCB** (Centre de Cultura Contemporània de Barcelona), a cultural centre with a vibrant programme of exhibitions. The centre, along with the square behind it, is a central part of the **Sónar Advanced**

Left: thrift shops line Raval's Carrer de la Riera Baixa.

housing was knocked down several years ago to create the broad **Rambla del Raval** ③, another move that was bitterly opposed at the time. Old residents and new immigrants are finally coming out into the sunshine to enjoy the space, and it is fast becoming a venue for lively outdoor markets and concerts.

## Towards the Waterfront

The tendrils of gentrification have not really reached much below the Carrer de Sant Pau, but there are a few noteworthy buildings worth visiting. On Sant Pau itself is the oldest church in the city, the Romanesque **Sant Pau del Camp**. Further down and towards La Rambla is Gaudí's medievalist **Palau Güell** ④. Currently being renovated, you can visit the ground floor and basement, but the rest of it is closed until at least the end of 2008. At the very bottom tip of the Raval is another handsome work of Catalan Gothic, the **Drassanes**, or Royal Shipyards. Nowadays the building houses the fascinating **Museu Marítim** ⑤ (Maritime Museum).

SEE ALSO CHURCHES, P.39; MODERNISME, P.81; MUSEUMS AND GALLERIES, P.88

Set into the wall of the **Casa de la Misericòrdia** is a small wooden circle. This is an old foundling wheel, where unwanted babies were pushed through and received by nuns on the other side until as recently as 1931.

**Music Festival** every June. The ripples of urban renewal have also spread to the surrounding streets, where galleries and designers' studios are rapidly opening.

SEE ALSO FESTIVALS, P.50; MUSEUMS AND GALLERIES, P.86–7

### Hospital de la Santa Creu ②

One of the few Gothic buildings of the *barrio*, the Hospital de la Santa Creu is a large complex that functioned as a hospital until the 1920s, and it was here that Gaudí was brought – and died – when he was hit by a tram. On the left is the 18th-century

**Academia de Medicina y Cirugía** (Academy of Medicine and Surgery), and on the right the **Institut d'Estudis Catalans** in the hospital's Casa de Convalescència. It has an atmospheric cloistered patio, a favourite with lounging students, tramps and, increasingly, the boho element of the *barrio*, thanks to the opening of a terrace café.

### Urban Regeneration

Just south of the old hospital is the site of the latest controversial move in urban regeneration. Rows of houses have been demolished, and a faceless apartment block erected, soon to be followed by a tall five-star hotel. More popular is the plan eventually to relocate the Generalitat's excellent rep cinema, the **Filmoteca** *(see p.53)*, here. To the west, another row of

**Right:** Sant Pau del Camp.
**Left:** skateboarder at MACBA.

# The Waterfront and Poblenou

It is ironic that this Mediterranean city, with a large industrial port and strong maritime tradition, gained a 'waterfront' only in the last decade of the 20th century. The vital catalyst for the rediscovery of the seafront was the 1992 Olympics, perhaps the most radical transformation of any city in Europe, and some 5 km (8 miles) of beaches were renovated or newly created, landscaped and equipped with facilities. The Vila Olímpica was also built, creating what is now a new residential district.

## Port Vell ①

The Port Vell (Old Port) was one of the waterfront areas to see massive transformation, most particularly with the addition of the **Maremàgnum** shopping centre and on another jetty beyond it, I.M. Pei's **World Trade Center**. Next to Maremàgnum is **L'Aquàrium**, one of Europe's largest, and the undervisited **IMAX** cinema. Back on the quayside, the promenade sweeps on round the marina to the former warehouse complex transformed into the **Palau de Mar** in 1992. This is a handsome building, very well renovated, and part of it now houses the

fascinating **Museu d'Història de Catalunya** ②. From here the **Passeig Joan de Borbó** is a cheerful strip of pubs, ice-cream parlours and paella restaurants aimed predominantly at tourists but all with sunny terraces. Serious eaters, meanwhile, tend to venture into the backstreets of Barceloneta.
SEE ALSO CHILDREN, P.36; FILM, P.53; MUSEUMS AND GALLERIES, P.88–9

## Barceloneta

Misleadingly called the Fishermen's Quarter, this area was in fact born of a political, military decision. It was to this area that the inhabitants of La

Ribera were relocated when their homes were demolished to make way for the building of Felipe V's citadel. The plans for Barceloneta were based on the construction of a series of narrow, rectangular blocks all facing in the same direction (towards the fortress), facilitating easy control. Today the diminutive nature of the apartments means that despite the desirable seaside location, the

The tall, rusted-looking stack of cubes on Barceloneta's beach is Rebecca Horn's *Estel Ferit* (Wounded Star), a homage to the *xiringuitos* (makeshift beach restaurants) that stood here.

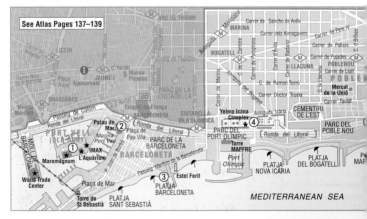

**Left:** the *Estel Ferit* (Wounded Star) sculpture *(see box, left)*.

warehouses and factories, the flats accommodated athletes in 1992 and since then have been gradually sold. Despite the attempts to create urban parks and sculpture, and the addition of a multiplex cinema (**Yelmo Icària Cineplex**), the area still feels somewhat lifeless, and holds little more than architectural interest.

SEE ALSO FILM, P.53

### Diagonal Mar

Diagonal Mar is the area where the Avinguda Diagonal cuts through the post-industrial neighbourhood of **Poblenou** and reaches the sea: old buildings and areas of wasteland are being transformed into vast apartment blocks. Several hotels and a huge shopping centre have opened, with further hotels still to come. Jutting out into the sea is the huge **Edifici Fòrum** ⑤, the legacy of the Universal Forum of Cultures, held in 2004 with the aim of promoting cultural diversity and a sustainable urban environment. The Fòrum grounds have become a site for large-scale events and will eventually include a new marina and an aquatic zoo.

SEE ALSO ARCHITECTURE, P.26;
SHOPPING, P.114

neighbourhood still has a local working-class feel.

### The Beaches

The stretch of beach here is actually three beaches, with different names, but most people know it as the **Platja Barceloneta** ③. Many fondly remember the *xiringuitos*, colourful restaurants, no more

than huts, that used to line it, and where you could eat good fish with your toes in the sand. They were bulldozed in the early 1990s under a cloud of controversy, but no one can deny the obvious pleasure the people of Barcelona derive from these wide-open beaches. Beyond the swish marina of the Port Olímpic are another five beaches. Tons of sand and hundreds of palm trees were imported to create **Platja Nova Icària**, **Bogatell**, **Mar Bella**, **Nova Mar Bella** and, most recently, **Llevant**.

SEE ALSO PARKS, GARDENS
AND BEACHES, P.100

### Vila Olímpica ④

The two skyscrapers and the copper fish sculpture by Frank Gehry rippling in the sun mark the entrance to the Vila Olímpica, or Olympic Village. Built on land formerly occupied by 19th-century

**Right:** the Platja Barceloneta.

# Montjuïc, Poble Sec and Sant Antoni

Known as a 'mountain', the rocky hill of Montjuïc is only 213 metres (699ft) high, but has an undeniable physical presence in the city; it also marks the end of the port, and acts like a barrier between the city centre and the industrial sprawl of the Zona Franca to the south. In 1929 the hill was landscaped and used as the grounds of the Universal Exposition. More recently, it was the nerve centre of the 1992 Olympic Games, and today it is a large city park offering a wide range of cultural, leisure and sporting activities.

## Gardens

Much of Montjuïc's verdant surface is given over to gardens. The newest is the **Jardí Botànic** ①, a sustainable botanic garden in keeping with Barcelona's aspirations for the new century. The plants and trees from around the world are slowly becoming established. Other thematic gardens include the **Jardins Costa i Llobera** (one of the biggest collections of cacti in the world) and the **Jardins Mossèn Cinto Verdaguer**, specialising in bulbous plants and ablaze with crocuses, daffodils and hyacinths in spring. More formally arranged are the **Jardins Laribal**, with their statuary and pretty rose garden, and the garden surrounding the **Grec** amphitheatre – a magical place to see a concert on a hot summer night.

SEE ALSO PARKS, GARDENS AND BEACHES, P.102

## Palau Nacional

From the Plaça Espanya, head past the twin Venetian-style towers that formed the main entrance to the Universal Exposition of 1929. Most of the buildings here were designed for this event, with a sweeping vista up to the

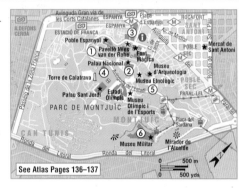

See Atlas Pages 136–137

Palau Nacional, the enormous, rather overbearing building at the top of the steps. Since 1934 it has housed the wonderful **MNAC** ② (Museu Nacional d'Art de Catalunya). In front is the imposing **Font Màgica**, the dancing fountain, which delights thousands of visitors several times a week during the *son et lumière* shows.

Off to one side is the minimalist **Pavelló Mies van der Rohe**. Built by Ludwig Mies van der Rohe as the German Pavilion for the 1929 Exhibition, it was later dismantled, but rebuilt in 1986 to celebrate the centenary of the architect's birth.

SEE ALSO ARCHITECTURE, P.26; CHILDREN, P.37; MUSEUMS AND GALLERIES, P.90

## CaixaForum and Poble Espanyol

Across the road is the Modernista Casaramona, originally a textile factory but now an excellent exhibition space, the **CaixaForum** ③. Further along the shady, green Avinguda del Marquès de Comillas is the **Poble Espanyol**, a 'Spanish village' with scaled-down versions of many of the country's most famous buildings. It also contains craft

> The **Refugi 307** (C/Nou de la Rambla 169; tel: 93 256 2122) is one of hundreds of bomb shelters built around Barcelona during the Spanish Civil War. This one, in Poble Sec, is now open to the public and holds a small museum.

**Left:** the Font Màgica's spectacular *son et lumière* show.

the top take the cable-car to the Castell de Montjuïc. The castle was built in the 17th century to control, rather than protect, the rebellious people of Barcelona, and is still unloved, although it is a handsome enough building, with a wide moat that serves as an outdoor cinema in summer. Descending from here on foot, you pass through the Plaça del Sardana with its circle of stone dancers, and the nearby Mirador de l'Alcalde lookout point, with panoramic views over the waterfront.

## Poble Sec and Sant Antoni

Boardering Montjuïc, Poble Sec and Sant Antoni are quiet, residential *barrios* with a slightly gentler pace than the rest of the Eixample. Good for a stroll, they also have some interesting and mostly tourist-free bars. Sant Antoni also has a pretty market, **Mercat de Sant Antoni**, with a fun second-hand book market on Sunday mornings.
SEE ALSO MARKETS, P.79

workshops, a good art gallery, restaurants and night-clubs, and stages some of the Festival del Grec's best concerts in summer.
SEE ALSO CHILDREN, P.37;
FESTIVALS, P.50; MUSEUMS AND
GALLERIES, P.89

### Olympic Ring ④

The **Anella Olímpica** (Olympic Ring) is spread across the hillside behind the Palau Nacional. The Estadi Olímpic was actually built for the 1929 Universal Exhibition, and then extended for the 1992 Olympics. Just outside the stadium is the new **Museu Olímpic i de l'Esport**, the first Olympic museum in Europe. Beyond the stadium to the right is the **Palau Sant Jordi**, now mostly used for rock concerts, and beyond that Santiago Calatrava's striking white communications tower, the **Torre de Calatrava**.
SEE ALSO MUSEUMS AND
GALLERIES, P.90

### Montjuïc's Museums

Montjuïc boasts a number of museums, but the most visited is the **Fundació Joan Miró** ⑤, in an understated yet powerfully impressive building designed by Miró's friend Josep Lluís Sert. As well as this and the splendid MNAC *(see left)*, there is a military museum (**Museu Militar**) in the castle and archaeological and ethnological museums (**Museu d'Arqueologia de Catalunya** and **Museu Etnològic**) on the lower slopes, towards the quiet neighbourhood of Poble Sec.
SEE ALSO MUSEUMS AND
GALLERIES, P.89–90

### Castell de Montjuïc ⑥

For the complete Montjuïc experience it's fun to take the funicular up the hill from Avinguda Paral·lel, and from

**Right:** view from Passeig de la Cascades by Palau Nacional.

# The Eixample

The origins of the Eixample (which means 'extension') lie in the 19th century, when civil engineer Ildefons Cerdà devised a clever way of expanding out of the Old City and subsuming the neighbourhoods such as Sants and Gràcia. Though political expediency took over in the end, his original idea was a utopian one; he planned a garden city for the working class in which only two of the four sides of each block would be built on, and the rest would provide green areas and shaded squares. In reality the blocks were built up on all sides, and bought by the wealthy upper classes, who commissioned many of the more fanciful works of Modernisme that adorn the area today.

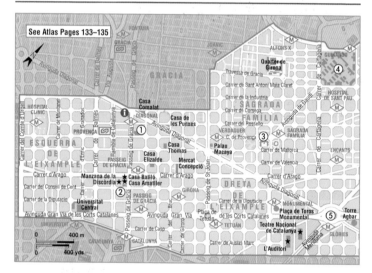

See Atlas Pages 133–135

### Passeig de Gràcia

This wide, tree-lined avenue originally linked the Old City and the outlying neighbourhood of Gràcia before it was integrated into Cerdà's plan and became the showground for some of the most spectacular Modernista buildings, such as Gaudí's **La Pedrera** ① apartment block, with its rippling grey stone façade. Intricate details abound on the street itself, from the hexagonal pavement tiles designed by Gaudí to the beautiful wrought-iron street lamps, incorporated with mosaic benches, which were designed by Pere Falqués in 1906.

SEE ALSO MODERNISME, P.82–3

The Eixample is generally known by its two halves, Esquerra (Left) and Dreta (Right). The Esquerra is more workaday and largely residential, while the Dreta holds most of the buildings of interest, along with offices, hotels and shopping. The dividing line is usually considered to be the Carrer de Balmes, once the site of the railway line that cut the district in two.

### MANZANA DE LA DISCÒRDIA

The most famous, and no doubt most visited, block on Passeig de Gràcia is between Consell de Cent and Aragó. The block, known as the Manzana de la Discòrdia, gained its name because of the close juxtaposition of three outstanding buildings, each of which is in a conflicting style, although they are all categorised as Modernista.

**Left:** the Sagrada Família.

At either end of the Rambla de Catalunya, parallel to Passeig de Gràcia, are two peculiar sculptures: *Meditation* – a cogitating bull – and *Coquette* – a reclining giraffe. Both are by sculptor Josep Granyer i Giralt and were put in place in 1972.

pavilions behind.
SEE ALSO CHURCHES, P.39; MODERNISME, P.82–3

### Plaça de les Glòries ⑤

Cerdà's original plan for the Eixample had the Plaça de les Glòries as its centre, something which current town planners are trying to resuscitate as an idea. For decades this has been an unloved area, housing nothing of interest but the city's tatty flea-market, a huge shopping centre and no shortage of traffic. In recent years, however, the addition of the neoclassical **Teatre Nacional de Catalunya**, the striking **L'Auditori** concert hall and the Jean Nouvel-designed **Torre Agbar** has changed that, and future plans to consolidate this as a cultural hub include a design museum and general pedestrianisation.
SEE ALSO ARCHITECTURE, P.27; MUSIC, P.92; THEATRE AND DANCE, P.124

The extravagantly sculpted **Casa Lleó Morera** ②, designed by Lluís Domènech i Montaner is on the corner, while slightly further up is the **Casa Amatller** by Josep Puig i Cadafalch, and next door to it is **Casa Batlló**, which was remodelled by Gaudí in 1906.
SEE ALSO MODERNISME, P.81–2

### Sagrada Família ③

The Eixample also contains the Sagrada Família, the symbol of Barcelona for many, and the reason the name **Antoni Gaudí** spread around the world. Here, in the centre of this bustling, ordinary neighbourhood, it is a staggering sight, its spires often likened to vast candles dripping wax in the heat. At the time of Gaudí's death in 1926 only the crypt, apse, the extraordinary Nativity façade and one tower had been completed. Today

there are eight spires in place, eventually to be joined by another 10. It is projected to be finished by 2026, though many feel this to be optimistic.

Along Avinguda de Gaudí is the much less known Modernista complex, the **Hospital Sant Pau** ④ (1902–12). Made up of over 20 buildings, it is the work of the prolific Domènech i Montaner. As it is a public hospital, you can wander through into the garden and

**Right:** Casa Lleó Morera, now a designer store.

19

# Upper Neighbourhoods

The vast majority of tourists never venture beyond the well-trodden paths of the Old City and the beach, with perhaps an occasional half-day spent at walking on Montjuïc or watching a football match at the Nou Camp. This only improves the lot of those that do, of course, ensuring that well-heeled Sarrià is ever peaceful and that beer in studenty Gràcia is ever affordable. It is not only these pockets of local colour that reward a metro ride, however – outside the centre are some of Barcelona's most interesting sights, from the monastery at Pedralbes to Gaudí's Park Güell.

### Park Güell ①

The second most visited park in Barcelona after the Ciutadella *(see p.100–1)*, Gaudí's Park Güell is a fantastical place, with fairytale gatehouses apparently sculpted from marshmallow, and an elegant esplanade lined with colourful undulating mosaic benches and giving a magnificent view over the city and out to sea. It was to have been a garden city, and the esplanade sits on top of what would have been the marketplace, supported by columns moulded like tall palm trees.
SEE ALSO MODERNISME, P.83; PARKS, GARDENS AND BEACHES, P.103

### Gràcia ②

Until the building of the Eixample in the 19th century, Gràcia was a separate town, and still has a very distinctive and down-to-earth character. Its streets are long, narrow and low-rise, and it buzzes with a youthful dynamism and is traditionally the neighbourhood of artisans, writers, artists and students. It also has an anarchic air and is a popular *barrio* with squatters and New Age aficionados. It is dotted with attractive plaças, such as the lively **Plaça del Sol**, which functions as an unofficial centre for the district. Nearby is the excellent **Verdi**

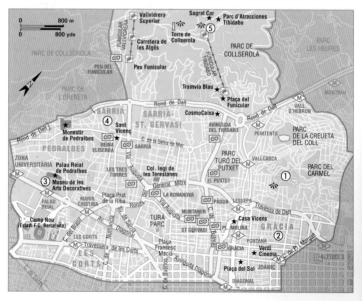

**Left:** the Monestir de Pedralbes.

village, with more charm than Pedralbes, and a more discreet display of wealth. This is a real neighbourhood with a soul: it has a market, café terraces and the attractive church of **Sant Vicenç** at the centre of things. The main street leading down from the church, **Major de Sarrià**, has been paved, encouraging strolling. From here passageways lead off through the backs of pretty Modernista villas with gardens bursting with bougainvillea.

## Tibidabo ⑤

The most enjoyable way to go up Tibidabo hill is on the **Tramvia Blau**. This blue wooden tram has been rattling up Avinguda Tibidabo, an avenue of beautiful Modernista houses, to the base of the Tibidabo funicular since 1901. The former elegance of Avinguda Tibidabo is now diminished, however, many of the large houses having been converted into institutions, advertising agencies or flats. The tram stops at the **Plaça del Funicular**, where you can enjoy the view with lunch or a drink, or you can catch a funicular to the summit and its old-fashioned funfair (**Parc d'Atraccions Tibidabo**).
SEE ALSO CHILDREN, P.37

cinema, one of the few places to show undubbed films.
SEE ALSO FILM, P.53

## Pedralbes

This exclusive neighbourhood, with manicured lawns, security guards and swimming pools, is not enormously characterful, but does contain the lovely **Monestir de Pedralbes**, a still functioning convent with an exquisitely elegant three-tiered Gothic cloister. A short walk down the Avinguda Pedralbes is the **Palau Reial de Pedralbes**, briefly the Barcelona residence for Alfonso XIII, and later for Franco. It now houses

> The **Casa Vicens** in Gràcia is one of Gaudí's early works, a neo-*mudéjar* fantasy of tiles and brickwork. It's a private residence and closed to the public, but is worth visiting for the façade. *See also Modernisme, p.83.*

> The church of **Sagrat Cor** atop the summit of Tibidabo is widely considered to be Barcelona's ugliest. Floodlit at night, however, it is magical from afar, and an emblematic part of the skyline, visible from all over the city.

the **Museu de Ceràmica** and **Museu de les Arts Decoratives** ③ (Museums of Ceramics and Decorative Arts), and will soon house the textile museum. Its formal gardens are worth a visit, as is the former lodge and snarling iron dragon on the gate, both designed by Gaudí. These are accessed along the side from the Avinguda Pedralbes.
SEE ALSO CHURCHES, P.39;
MUSEUMS AND GALLERIES, P.91

## Sarrià ④

Another of the sought-after uptown areas, Sarrià is still recognisable as a former

**Right:** benches in Park Güell.

# Around Barcelona

B arcelona has enough to satisfy the most demanding of holidaymakers, but for those that need a break from the hustle and bustle of city life (or simply a cleaner stretch of sand), the Catalan hinterland and long stretches of coastline on either side of Barcelona provide some exceptional opportunities for excursions from the city, and most are possible on public transport. As well as the beaches and low mountains such as Montserrat or the Collserola range mentioned below, there are the rolling vineyards of the Penedès and the grand historic cities of Tarragona and Girona all within just a short ride. *See also Excursions, p.42–3.*

which merits the trip alone, with its cave-like interior, sinuous pillars and butterfly-inspired stained-glass windows.

## Garraf and Sitges

The closest clean and uncrowded beach to the city is **Garraf** ③, an easy train ride down south. Here you will find a peaceful little bay ringed with wooden beach huts, along with a couple of simple restaurants. For a bit more life, however, you need to continue south for another 10 minutes or so, to arrive at **Sitges** ④, with its gleaming, whitewashed houses and flower-festooned balconies. An international party atmosphere pervades Sitges in summer, and the

## Collserola ①

The Collserola hills form a green belt of pine and holm oak spreading to Sant Cugat and beyond. On the other side of Tibidabo, away from the city, it is another world, a mere 15-minute train ride from Plaça Catalunya to Baixador de Vallvidrera station. Walk up a well-landscaped path to the Centre d'Informació del Parc de Collserola, the information centre (daily 9.30am–3pm): a helpful base with an exhibition about the wildlife in the natural park, maps, advice and a bar/restaurant.

SEE ALSO WALKS AND TOURS, P.128

## Colònia Güell ②

One easy trip which can be done in half a day or less is a visit to **Santa Coloma de Cervelló** to see the Colònia Güell, another attempt, like the Park Güell, to build a garden city for the workers, in this case of Eusebi Güell's textile factory. As with the park, Güell enlisted the help of his friend Antoni Gaudí, but the only part that Gaudí managed to complete was the crypt of the church,

**Right:** stained-glass detail and sanctuary buildings at Montserrat.

## Costa Maresme

The beaches just north of Barcelona have a much lower profile than Sitges, and are much maligned for the railway line that runs alongside them. As a result, they are often less crowded. In recent years most have been overhauled, with some beaches being widened, promenades landscaped and marinas built. One of the most attractive resorts is **Caldes d'Estrac** ⑤, also known as Caldetes. It is a spa town – several hotels have thermal baths – with many charms and pretty Modernista houses. The long, sandy beaches never seem to get too crowded, and the sea is usually clear. The beaches of Caldetes merge with those of **Arenys de Mar**, known for its attractive fishing port. Further up this coast is Sant Pol, a pretty, whitewashed fishing village with a lively beachfront.

> Montserrat monastery's famous Escolans, the oldest boys' choir in Europe, sings every day at 1pm during Mass. To catch them, be prepared to queue, or take advantage of the sudden lull and explore the area around the monastery in peace.

town has a full calendar of festivals year-round, including a notoriously wild Carnival. Fringed by palms and populated by an intriguingly diverse range of bathers, including a large gay community, the gently curving Platja d'Or (Golden Beach) runs from the 17th-century Església Sant Bartomeu i Santa Tecla, perched on the headland, and extends 5km (3 miles) south and west past the Hotel Terramar. The beaches on the other side of the church are also worth exploring.

## Montserrat ⑥

Catalonia's most important religious site is the monastery atop the Montserrat mountain, reached by train plus cable car or cogwheel railway from Plaça Espanya. There is a separate door at the front of the basilica for people wanting to see and touch the statue of Madonna and Child, but be prepared to queue. The basilica is packed with works of art by prominent painters and sculptors, including paintings by El Greco in the sanctuary's museum. Catalan poets have dedicated some of their most inspired verse to Montserrat, while Goethe is said to have dreamt of it, and Parsifal sought the Holy Grail here in Wagner's opera.

23

# A–Z

In the following section the city's attractions and services are organised by theme, under alphabetical headings. Items that link to another theme are cross-referenced. All sights that fall within the bounds of the atlas section at the end of the book are given a page number and grid reference.

# Architecture

Barcelona is one of the architecturally proudest cities in Europe, boasting over 2,000 years of town planning. Chunks of ancient stone wall from Roman Barcino give perspective, while the maze-like lanes of the Barri Gòtic *(see p.8–9)* and the Call (the Jewish quarter) are great for exploring. Flanking the Old Town, the Eixample *(see p.18–19)* is a piece of visionary urban design by the engineer Ildefons Cerdà. New areas like Diagonal Mar *(see p.15)* boast a distinctly Manhattan-style skyline, with world-famous architects like Calatrava, Foster and Rogers clamouring to put their buildings here. *See also Modernisme, p.80–3.*

### Edifici Fòrum

Avda Diagonal with Rambla Prim, Poblenou; tel: 93 230 1000; metro: Maresme Fòrum
Celebrity architects **Herzog** and **de Meuron** came up with the 'blue' building for the Universal Forum of Cultures in 2004. Like most things in this city, it has taken a while for folks to warm to it, but the building is strikingly impressive, seeming to hover above the earth like a lost space-ship. Water covers the roof and gives an underwater aspect to the interior, but the bleak tarmac surrounding it is perhaps a little too urban for most tastes. The new beach and offshore island for sun-bathing lighten the mood, however, and the complex is now the host of several music festivals through the year.

### Gas Natural

Plaça del Gas 1, Waterfront; metro: Barceloneta; map p.138 B4
The new gas headquarters located just next to the Hotel Arts *(see p.68)* is probably the city's most exciting new build. It has several parts shooting off a central skyscraper and is

**Antoni Gaudí** is Barcelona's most famous architect *(see also Modernisme, p.80–3),* but his contemporary equivalents the late **Enric Miralles** and his long-time partner **Benedetta Tagliabue** are just as deserving of fame. Their fingerprints are evident on much of the city's best recent architecture, including the colourful acoustic panels on the Gran Via that prevent traffic noise reaching nearby housing; the billowing-roofed Santa Caterina market *(see p.79)*; the rippling 'Lungo-mare' bench; as well as those mentioned below.

completely made out of glass, but despite the high-tech lines, its integration with the old fishing quarter of Barceloneta and the shoreline appears seamless. Add to that a consciousness for creating interesting and high-quality urban public spaces, and it's no wonder locals like it.

### Parc de les Tres Xemeneies

Avda del Paral·lel 51–55, Poble Sec; metro: Paral·lel;

map p.137 E2
Built in the first years of the 1990s, this is another odd one, but a treat for lovers of industrial architecture. Three tall red-brick chimneys add drama to an otherwise ordinary-looking concrete-and-glass office block. In the foreground a sheet of black water reflects the whole, believed to be a 3D interpretation of a painting by Giorgia de Chirico, who specialised in power stations.

### Pavelló Mies van der Rohe

Avda Marquès de Comillas, Montjuïc; tel: 93 423 4016; www.miesbcn.com; daily 10am–8pm; admission charge; metro: Plaça Espanya; map p.136 B4
This wonderfully light and airy construction with its glass-and-marble walls, and a 'floor' of water overlooked by a replica of Georg Kolbe's bronze sculpture of *Alba* (Dawn), is one of Barcelona's great modernist (not to be confused with Modernisme)

**Right:** interior and exterior of the Edifici Fòrum.

**Left:** the Torre Agbar at night.

controversial building to go up in recent years. Commissioned by the Barcelona Water Board, the gherkin-shaped structure is made of glass and concrete, and lit by multi-coloured mood-lighting at night. For now it remains off-limits to the public, but opinion is warming, and it is well worth taking a gander from one of the cross-streets like C/Casp in the Eixample Dreta, or from Els Encants market. Get too close and you kind of miss it.

### Torre de Collserola

Ctra de Vallvidrera al Tibidabo; tel: 93 406 9354; www.torre decollserola.com; Apr–June, Sept: Wed–Fri 11am–2.30pm, Sat–Sun until 7pm, Aug: daily 11am–2.30pm, 3.30–8pm, Oct–Mar: daily 11am–2.30pm; admission charge; FCG: Peu Funicular, then Funicular

Norman Foster's extraordinary communications tower perches on top of the Collserola mountain range rather like a toothpick in a tapa. What most people do not realise is that you can take a knuckle-biting glass-elevator ride to the top. Nowhere beats it for a view over Barcelona, and the signs indicating distance to the rest of the world's great cities add useful dinner-party trivia to the experience.

buildings. Built for the 1929 World Exhibition, the original was destroyed after the event, but what stands on the space now is a fine replica and increasingly popular for glamorous parties.

### Pont Bac de la Roda

Pont Felip II-Bac de Roda s/n, Sagrera; FCG: Navas

To get to **Santiago Calatrava**'s futuristic bridge you need to take an FCG train from Plaça Catalunya to Navas station in La Sagrera, which promises to reach its own architecturally omnipotent heights in the next few years with a new transport hub for the new high-speed AVE train. At 10 metres (33ft) high and 129 metres (423ft) long, what it lacks in grandeur it makes up for in magic. The swooping, gleaming white arches against a piercing blue sky give a sense of flying, and the fact that this impressive gesture was built to connect two of the city's poorer neighbourhoods shows inspired thinking in raising the spirits of the community.

### Torre Agbar

Plaça de les Glòries, Eixample; metro: Glòries; map p.135 E1

Jean Nouvel's distinctly phallic office block has been the most

# Bars and Cafés

*B*arcelonins are a sociable lot. They love nothing better than a get-together on one of the city's many terraces, or to crowd into bars after work for a *cervesa*, cava or cocktail. Visitors will find it is one of the most convivial places on earth for imbibing the good stuff, with venues ranging from beautiful Modernisme cafés for atmospheric breakfasts, to super-cool lounge bars. In Spain it is considered fairly uncouth to drink without eating, and so, with the exception of a handful of cocktail bars, nearly all of those listed offer some form of sustenance. *See also Nightlife, p.94–7, Restaurants, p.104–13 and Tapas Bars, p.120–3.*

### Plaça de Catalunya and La Rambla

#### Boadas
C/Tallers 1; tel: 93 318 9592; Mon–Sat noon–2am; metro: Plaça de Catalunya; map p.138 B4
A legend in its own right, Boadas was the brainchild of Miguel Boadas, the son of Catalan immigrants who had worked at Hemingway's famous haunt, El Floridita in Havana. Deciding Barcelona could do with a cocktail bar of its own, he returned in the 1930s and opened this diminutive Art Deco space to loud cheers from the locals. Since then the great and the good have all enjoyed mojitos and martinis here, notably George Orwell, Sophia Loren and artist Joan Miró.

#### Café de l'Òpera
La Rambla 74; tel: 93 317 7585; www.cafeoperabcn.com; daily 8.30am–2am; metro: Liceu or Plaça de Catalunya; map p.138 B3
Opened in the 18th century as a tavern servicing carriages leaving for Madrid and Zaragoza, the Café de l'Òpera was refurbished in the mid-19th century in the Viennese style with wood panelling, chandeliers and decorative mirrors. Since it opened in 1929 it has never once shut – not even during the Civil War – and continues to serve a great hot chocolate.

#### Pastelería Escribá
Rambla de les Flors 81; tel: 93 301 6027; www.escriba.es; daily 8.30am–9pm; metro: Liceu; map p.138 B3
The elaborate Art Nouveau decorations of colourful floral mosaic work and stained glass at this iconic café were done in 1902 by the stage designer Ros i Güell, and make a suitably whimsical backdrop to the decadent cakes and pastries. The candy jewellery makes an unusual gift, and the leafy patio is a great escape from the bustle of the market.

**Left:** the drinks menu at La Vinya del Senyor.

## Viena

La Rambla 115; tel: 93 317 1492; Mon–Fri 8am–1.30am, Sat 8am–2am, Sun 8am–12.30am; metro: Plaça de Catalunya; map p.138 B4

An article in the *New York Times* recently declared Viena's *flauta de jamón iberico* the best in the world. Fresco ceilings and a finger-shaped bar given it luxe factor, while bottles of HP and Worcester sauce keep it real. The secret is in the dough for the *flautas*, which are fermented for 24 hours to give a crisp crust and a chewy centre.

## Zurich

Plaça de Catalunya 1; tel: 93 317 9153; May–Oct: Mon–Fri 8am–1am, Sat–Sun 10am–1am, Nov–Apr: Mon–Fri 8am–11pm, Sat–Sun 8am–midnight; metro: Plaça de Catalunya; map p.138 B4

Good as a central meeting spot, Zurich is fine for watching the world go by, but as a destination it has had its day. The interior is still handsome enough, but the crowds that

**Left:** fried *churros* and hot chocolate at La Granja.

pass through mean service can be slow and disinterested.

## Barri Gòtic

### The Bagel Shop

C/Canuda 25; tel: 93 302 4161; Mon–Sat 9.30am–9.30pm, Sun 11am–4pm; metro: Jaume I or Plaça de Catalunya; map p.138 B4

The only bagel shop worth its salt in the city; its authentic, chewy dough rings come in a myriad of flavours and interesting toppings. If you want to bulk-buy for take-out breakfast at the weekend, call a day ahead.

### Caelum

C/de la Palla 8; tel: 93 302 6993; Mon 5–8.30pm, Tue–Thur 10.30am–8.30pm, Fri–Sat 10.30am–midnight, Sun 11am–3pm; metro: Jaume I; map p.138 B4

Most things in this tearoom-cum-cake shop were made by nuns and monks from all over Spain. The arcaded basement dining room occupies the former Jewish women's baths and is a good place to sample chocolate figs doused in brandy and marzipan treats.

## Ginger

C/Palma de Sant Just 1; tel: 93 310 5309; Tue–Thur 7pm–2.30am, Fri–Sat 7pm–3am; metro: Jaume I; map p.138 B3

An un-self-consciously trendy hang-out with a wine bar at one end and a cocktail bar at the other. Regulars sprawl over sofas and armchairs in the various lounges picking at top-flight snacks such as grilled *fetge* with candied apples and tuna with sesame and ginger.

## La Granja

C/de Banys Nous 4; tel: 93 302 6975; Mon–Sat 9.30am–2pm, 5–9pm; metro: Jaume I; map p.138 B3

Open since 1872, this is the loveliest of the old city's *granjas* (dairies) specialising in custard-thick hot

chocolate. With modernity has come a demand for refreshments a little less artery-clogging, and so while you admire the Modernista décor contrasted by a section of Roman murals, you can also sip on herbal teas and more moderate coffees.

## Sant Pere and Born

### La Vinya del Senyor
Plaça Santa Maria 5; tel: 93 310 3379; Mon–Thur noon–1am,

Fri–Sat noon–2am, Sun noon–midnight; metro: Jaume I; map p.138 C2

Looking straight onto Santa Maria del Mar *(see p.38–9)*, this is the hottest little wine bar in town. It offers a magnificent range of Spanish and Catalan labels, many by the glass, accompanied by delectable tapas.

### Pisamorena
C/Consolat de Mar; no phone; Mon–Thur, Sun 9am–12.30am, Fri–Sat 10.30am–1am; metro: Barceloneta; map p.138 B2

A taste of the south in the north, Pisamorena adds a mixed bag to its peaceful terrace and cute bar. Most come for the *fino* (crisp, dry sherry from Andalusia), toasted almonds and olives, and the eerie wail of flamenco.

### Pony
C/Portal Nou 23; no phone; Mon, Wed–Sun 6pm–2am; metro: Arc de Triomf; map p.139 C3

A rash of openings on this Born side-street have recently put it in direct competition with Raval's Joaquim Costa *(see box above)* for coolness. Pony is little more than a corridor painted red, black and gold, but the groovers and shakers adore it, not least for occasional lock-ins. World music and dangerously cheap drinks second the vote.

### Rococó
C/Gombau 5–7; tel: 660 591 755/658 028 580; Mon–Thur 9am–midnight, Fri 9am–3am, Sat 10am–3am; metro: Jaume I; map p.138 C3

Delightful café serving excellent java, Vietnamese rolls and salads by day, hip cocktail bar by night. The distinctly French-Caribbean flavour gives it added sparkle.

### El Xampanyet
C/Montcada 22; tel: 93 319 7003; Tue–Sat noon–4pm and

7–11.30pm; metro: Jaume I; map p.138 C3

A pretty, ceramic-tiled *xampañería* (cava bar) serving a sweetish own-brand fizz alongside tiny peppers stuffed with goats cheese, slivers of *jamón* and famous home-cured anchovies. Look no further if you're seeking the quintessential Barcelona experience.

## Raval

### Indian Lounge
C/Sant Ramon 23; no phone; Mon–Thur 6pm–midnight, Fri–Sat 10pm–3am; metro: Liceu and Paral·lel; map p.138 A3

A sign of the new generation immigrants starting to make their mark in the city, this relative newcomer to the *barrio* oozes oriental sensuality. The chill-out lounge dotted with candles and incense is as good a place as any to get cosy with the house special: a hukka pipe infused with absinthe.

### It Café
C/Joaquim Costa 4; tel: 93 443 0341; Mon–Wed 5pm–1.30am, Thur 5pm–2.30am, Fri–Sat 5pm–3am, Sun 5pm–midnight; metro: Liceu or Universitat; map p.137 E4

Finding a sofa in this town can be elusive, so this home-style lounge-bar is a bonus for those who like drinking in comfort. There's a certain hippy ambience to the place, with regular art and photography exhibitions of variable quality, but the open-armed policy gives it a warm, fuzzy feel that is rare.

### Kentucky
C/Arc del Teatre 11; tel: 93 318 2878; Wed–Sat 10pm–3.30am; metro: Drassanes; map p.138 A2

From that lost era when bars were just bars, Kentucky is

**Right:** La Vinya del Senyor.

### La Penúltima
C/Riera Alta 40; no phone;
Tue–Sun 7pm–3am; metro: Sant
Antoni; map p.137 E4

Good for a nightcap, or for a
first cap for that matter,
anything goes at this quirky
little bar with its bizarre ever-
changing window decorations.
Lined by barrels out front with
mismatched tables and chairs
out back, it does good-value
wines by the bottle (the house
stuff requires guts of steel) to
accompany mixed boards of
cheese and charcuterie.

### Resolis
C/Riera Baixa 22; tel: 93 441
2948; Mon–Sat 11am–midnight;
metro: Sant Antoni, Universitat
or Liceu; map p.138 A4

A little bit country, a little bit
rock and roll, this popular but
largely unknown watering hole
can be found on a second-
hand and vintage-clothing
shopping lane. An outdoor bar
serves cold beers, creative
tapas like ceviche, and quality
wines through the summer.

### The Waterfront and Poblenou

### CDLC
Passeig Marítim 32; tel: 93 224
0407; www.cdlcbarcelona.com;
daily noon–3am; metro:
Ciutadella-Vila Olímpica or
Barceloneta; map p.139 D1

under no illusions: dark,
sweaty and in desperate
need of an overhaul, it is
nevertheless one of the most
fun nights out in town. Usually a very drunken one
when punters hit the tiny
dance floor for a final fling
before dawn.

### Lletraferit
C/Joaquim Costa 43; tel: 93 301
1961; Mon–Thur 4pm–2.30am,
Fri–Sat 4pm–3am; metro: Universitat or Sant Antoni; map
p.137 E4

Ah, civilisation at last.
There's something very
Greenwich Village about this
spot, with its loft-style interior, black leather sofas and
bookcases. A brilliant nook
for working and reading in
the afternoon, a quiet place
away from the mayhem for a
cocktail and conversation
at night.

Seize the night is the maxim that people live by at this super-sexy Morocco-meets-Bali-themed beach club. Book well in advance if you want to make use of the vast day beds beloved by VIPs and visiting celebs. Otherwise get here early to earn your place on the terrace. Once into the bowels of the place, it is every man for himself.

### Ice Barcelona

C/Ramon Trias Fargas 2; tel: 93 224 1625; www.icebarcelona.com; Mon–Sun 8pm–2.30am; metro: Ciutadella-Vila Olímpica; map p.139 D1

No excuses for being too hot now with the arrival of the city's first ice-bar. Like everywhere else where everything from the bar to the glasses are carved from frozen *agua* you'll probably only want to go once, but the terrace does offer a reprise.

### Sal Café

Passeig Marítim s/n; tel: 93 224 0707; Tue–Sun noon–5pm, 8.30pm–1am, Thur–Sat until 3am; metro: Barceloneta; map p.139 D1

Snag a seat at the bar to appreciate the best Mediterranean views at this casually fashionable beachside spot. The terrace rocks in the summer, but it has its own special vibe during the cooler months when surfers, regular visitors and locals all get together without the onslaught of summer revellers.

### Santa Marta

C/Grau I Torras 59; no phone; daily 10.30am–12.30am, Fri–Sat until 1am; metro: Barceloneta; map p.138 C1

Lively and bustling, this bijou Italian hang-out seems like it is constantly on the verge of breaking out into a party. Lunchtime sandwiches and salads are only average, but its authentic Venetian Spritz cocktails and *tremezzini* (retro triangular finger sandwiches) cannot be beaten.

### El Tio Che

Rambla de Poble Nou 44–46; tel: 93 309 1872; www.eltioche.com; Mon–Thur, Sun 10am–1pm, Fri–Sat 10am–3pm; metro: Poblenou

Open since 1912, this pretty, tiled café is something of a Barcelona institution despite being so far off the beaten path. Folks travel from all over town to stroll down the 'other' Ramblas and sip on cool beakers of Uncle Che's refreshing *horchata* (sweet tiger-nut milk). It is a handy stop pre- or post-beach.

### Vaixell de Luz de Gas

Moll del Diposit s/n; tel: 93 484 2326; Mar–May, Sept–Oct: daily noon–8pm, June–Aug: daily noon–3am; metro: Barceloneta; map p.138 C2

There is something hugely luxurious about boat parties, and if you cannot afford your own, you can at least join this one. Permanently moored in the north end of the Port Vell, this one has upper and lower decks where folks soak up the sun and drink copious amounts of white wine and cava.

## Montjuïc, Poble Sec and Sant Antoni

### Bar Seco

Passeig de Montjuïc 74; tel: 93 329 6374; daily 11am–2am; metro: Paral·lel; map p.137 D2

The spiritual home of Barcelona's slow-food movement, this pint-sized bar and restaurant specialises in local produce and organic Catalan beers with a dinner menu to

**Right:** the twinkling Xix Bar.

match. Great in the summer when high tables spill onto the pavement.

### La Caseta del Migdia
C/Mirador de Migdia s/n; tel: 617 956 572; www.lacaseta.org; Oct–May: Sat–Sun 10am–7pm, June–Sept: Thur–Sat 6pm–2.30am, Sun 10am–1am; metro: Plaça de Espanya then bus 55, or Funicular from Paral·lel to Montjuïc, or walk; map p.136 B1

A hike up the mountain rewards with this fabulous little retreat. La Caseta is an abandoned house reclaimed as a bar nested in the forest of Montjuïc with mesmerising sea views. There is a BBQ and funky DJs at weekends through the summer.

### Cerveseria Jazz
C/Margarit 43; no phone; Tue–Thur 7pm–2am, Fri–Sat 7pm–3am; metro: Poble Sec; map p.137 D3

As the name suggests, the soul of this place comes from well-chosen jazz and blues numbers and a veritable shrine to the genre on the walls. But it is famous for its beer and burgers, which are arguably the best in town.

### The Pastry Shop
C/Villarroel 22; tel: 93 424 0204; www.thepastryshop.es; Mon 4–11pm, Tue–Wed 1.30–11pm, Thur–Fri 1.30pm–midnight, Sat 6pm–2am; metro: Urgell; map p.137 E4

An American-style café in this quiet and leafy *barrio*, The Pastry Shop is a good choice for light lunches or afternoon tea. Particularly good are the home-made muffins, carrot and chocolate cake as well as heartier staples like soups, sandwiches and salads.

### Xix Bar
C/Rocafort 19; tel: 93 423 4314; www.xixbar.com; daily 6.30pm–3am; metro: Poble Sec; map p.137 D3

This converted dairy dazzles with fairy-lights and charming service, and has made its name thanks to a mind-boggling array of gourmet gin and tonics. Owner Mike Cruickshank is famous for his

**Left and below:** Dry Martini's expert bar staff.

### Dry Martini

C/Aribau 162–166; tel: 93 217 5072; Mon–Thur 1pm–2.30am, Fri 1pm–3am, Sat 6.30pm–3am, Sun 6pm–2.30am; FGC: Provença; map p.134 A3

The mother of all Barcelona's cocktail bars; the wood panelling, bottle-green armchairs and antique bottles give a suitably decadent air to the city's best Martini makers. There is also a clandestine restaurant called Speakeasy tucked away in the stock warehouse offering top-fight Mediterranean fare.

### Mayura

C/de Girona 57; tel: 93 481 4536; www.mayuralounge.es; Mon–Thur 1–4pm, 8.30pm–2am, Fri 1–4pm, 8.30pm–3am, Sat 8.30pm–3am; metro: Girona; map p.134 C1

Better for drinks than for dinner, this Indian-themed lounge bar has a Zen-like twist with its water features, pebbles and bamboo scattered among the silken sofas. The wood-and-slate bar, for example, has a water channel bobbing with candles and flowers, and the drinks list reads like a Bollywood film festival: Delhi Ditz anyone?

### Pastisseries Mauri

Rambla de Catalunya 102; tel:

ritualistic cocktail-making skills, painstakingly dripping fresh lime oils into a goldfish bowl of Hendrick's gin, cucumber slices and tonic. No need for doubles here.

### The Eixample

**Bauma**

C/Roger de Llúria 124; tel: 93 459 0566; Mon–Fri, Sun 8am–midnight; metro: Diagonal; map p.134 B3

This old-school café dating back to the 1940s is totally Brooklyn, with its ancient red banquettes and soothing Sunday-morning sounds. Pick up a paper on the Ramblas and settle in to nurse the inevitable hangover away.

**Right:** Café del Sol, a Gràcia favourite.

93 215 8146; Mon–Sat 9am–2pm, 4–7pm; metro: Diagonal; map p.134 B3

The ultimate in high-class tea salons, this place is full of glam grannies in pearls, the *pijo* (posh) set and accidental tourists. Waiters in smart white gloves dole out dainty sandwiches with the crusts cut off and gorgeous little cakes.

## Upper Neighbourhoods

### Café del Sol
Plaça del Sol 16; tel: 93 414 5663; Mon–Thur noon–2.30am, Fri–Sat noon–3am; metro: Fontana; map p.134 B3

A Gràcia institution where students gather to drink beer, pump and grind to the eclectic mix of music within and generally make a racket on the square. Nobody seems to mind; anything goes in this hip alternative *barrio*.

### Café Viennese
Passeig de Gràcia 132; tel: 93 255 3000; www.hotelcasafuster.com; Sun–Wed 9am–2am, Thur–Sat 9am–3am; metro: Diagonal; map p.134 B3

It will cost you an arm and a leg to have anything in this elaborately decorated tearoom, but the sumptuous wine-coloured sofas and gold-flecked marble pillars in this magnificently restored Domènech i Montaner build-

In the summer Barcelona's beaches hot up when the *Xiringuitos* (beach bars) open their hatches, chill down the beer and turn up the stereo. While Barceloneta's bars shut down fairly early, those beyond the Port Olímpic all the way up to Bogatell (the beach in front of Poblenou) sizzle the minute the sun goes down.

ing make it a right royal experience. Also lovely for a glass of wine in the evening if you're heading uptown.

### Mirabé
C/Manuel Arnús 2; tel: 93 418 5667; Mon–Sat 7pm–3am, Sun 4pm–2am; metro: Tibidabo then Tramvia Blau

Boasting the best views in town, Mirabé has great wraparound windows to make the most of it, with a fantastic wood-decked terrace and garden that opens up in spring

and summer. If it is too posh for you, its little sister, Mirablau next door, has the same views and a more basic terrace.

### La Nena
C/de Ramón y Cajal 36; tel: 93 285 1476; Oct–July: daily 9am–10pm, Aug and Sept: 9am–2pm, 4–10pm; metro: Fontana or Joanic; map p.134 C4

Sugar and spice and all things nice, that's what small and lovely *La Nena*, or the little girl in English, is made of. Go for breakfast or afternoon tea.

# Children

Spain is famously child-friendly, and there are few places where kids are excluded. Babies and toddlers, particularly, are a great cultural ice-breaker, and you can expect yours to attract plenty of friendly attention. Spanish children are allowed to stay up much later than elsewhere, particularly in the summer, when no one bats an eyelid at children having dinner in restaurants. As well as the attractions listed below, the living statues and street performers along La Rambla *(see p.6–7)* are usually a hit, along with the boats in the Port Vell *(see p.14–5)* and the cable-cars running across the port and up to Montjuïc castle *(see p.17).*

## Accommodation

All but the very cheapest *pensiones* should be able to provide a cot *(cuna)* for babies, and will not usually charge for it.

## Babysitting

**Tender Loving Canguros**
Tel: 647 605 989; www.tlcanguros.com
English-speaking babysitters available on short- or long-term basis. Fees begin at €7 per hour plus agency fee.

## Museums

**CosmoCaixa**
C/Teodor Roviralta 47–51, Tibidabo; tel: 93 212 6050; www.fundaciolacaixa.es; Tue–Sun 10am–8pm; admission charge; FGC: Avda Tibidabo
A sizeable science museum with especially good interactive exhibits for children, along with a patch of 'Amazonian forest', inhabited by 100 species of flora and fauna, that they can walk through.
SEE ALSO MUSEUMS AND GALLERIES, P.91

**Museu de Cera
(Wax Museum)**
Passatge de la Banca 7, Barri

Gòtic; tel: 93 317 2649; www.museocerabcn.com; summer: daily 10am–10pm, winter: Mon–Fri 10am–1.30pm, 4–7.30pm, Sat–Sun 11am–2pm, 4.30–8.30pm; admission charge; metro: Drassanes; map p.138 A2
Superman sits atop the roof of Barcelona's wax museum, poised to leap, and inside are another 360 or so waxworks, giving an insight into some of Catalonia's historic personalities, along with famous faces from films, books and popular culture everywhere.

**Museu de la Xocolata
(Chocolate Museum)**
C/del Comerç 36; tel: 93 268

7878; www.pastisseria.cat; Mon, Wed–Sat 10am–7pm, Sun 10am–3pm; admission charge; metro: Jaume I; map p.139 C3
Another museum that, while not specifically for children, has an inevitable appeal for the little ones. The scaled chocolate models of famous buildings and cartoon characters are especially popular.
SEE ALSO MUSEUMS AND GALLERIES, P.86

## Other Attractions

**L'Aquàrium**
Moll d'Espanya; tel: 93 221 7474; www.aquariumbcn.com; July–Aug: daily 9.30am–11pm, Sept–June: 9.30am–9pm; admission

**Left:** playing on the swings at the Parc de la Ciutadella.

metro: Barceloneta/Ciutadella–Vila Olímpica; map p.139 C2

A good-sized zoo with all the usual suspects: elephants, giraffes, bears, hippos, rhinos and so on. There's also a farmyard corner where children can stroke the animals, and – at weekends – pony rides. Another favourite attraction is the dolphin show.

## Parks and Playgrounds

Many of the city squares and parks have playgrounds for the under-fives, with swings, slides and seesaws. Especially child-friendly parks are **Ciutadella**, which has two playgrounds and a boating lake; **Parc del Castell de l'Oreneta**, with pony rides and a mini-train; and **Parc del Laberint**, which has a maze. SEE ALSO PARKS, GARDENS AND BEACHES, P.100, 103

> The ludoteca at the **Parc de la Ciutadella** (see p.100) is great way to cheer up bored toddlers. Every day at 11am–2pm and 4.30–6.30pm (later in summer), monitors bring out Wendy houses, trikes, knee-high cars, buckets and spades and assorted plastic toys into the playground for kids to play with, free of charge (pictured below).

charge; metro: Barceloneta/Drassanes; map p.138 B1

One of the largest in Europe, Barcelona's aquarium is looking a little tatty at the edges these days, but is still fun. Its biggest attraction is the glass tunnel running through the shark tank, though small children also love the interactive exhibits upstairs in the Explora! section or the underwater antics of the Humboldt penguins in Planeta Aqua.

## Font Màgica (Magic Fountain)

Plaça Carles Buïgas 1, Montjuïc; tel: 93 291 4036; free; metro: Espanya; map p.136 B4

Spain's ongoing drought has curtailed the performances of the Magic Fountain in 2008, but you can still catch the surging jets, pounding music and kaleidoscopic lighting every night from Thursday to Sunday in summer and Friday and Saturday in winter.

## Parc d'Atraccions Tibidabo (Funfair)

Plaça del Tibidabo; tel: 93 211 79 42; www.tibidabo.es; opening hours vary: see

website; admission charge; FGC Avda Tibidabo, then bus or tram to Plaça Doctor Andreu, then funicular

Tibidabo's funfair has been the city's playground for over 100 years now, and consequently its rides range from ancient to bleeding-edge. There is also a museum of delightfully antiquated automata, puppet show and circus performances.

## Poble Espanyol

Avda Marquès de Comillas 13, Montjuïc; tel: 93 325 7866; www.poble-espanyol.com; Sun 9am–midnight, Mon 9am–8pm, Tue–Thur 9am–2am, Fri–Sat 9am–4am; admission charge; metro: Espanya; map p.136 B4

A fake village, where kids can run around with no fear of traffic, visit craft studios, attend workshops and story-telling sessions and follow a clue-solving route, treasure-hunt-style.

## Zoo

Parc de la Ciutadella; tel: 93 225 6780; www.zoobarcelona.com; mid-Mar–May, Oct: daily 10am–6pm, June–Sept: daily 10am–7pm, Nov–March: daily 10am–5pm; admission charge;

**Left:** L'Aquàrium's shark tank.

# Churches

Spain's Desamortización (Disentailment) of monasteries in 1836 saw many destroyed or sold, and in the Setmana Tràgica (Tragic Week) of rioting in 1909 many churches and monasteries went up in flames, often with the clergy trapped inside. For all that, many stunning examples have survived. Below is a handful of the more interesting, but also worth visiting are Santa Anna (C/Santa Anna) for its hidden Gothic cloister; Santa Maria del Pi, on the square of the same name, for its vast rose window; and the Església de Betlem (La Rambla with C/Carme) for its elaborate baroque façade.

## Barri Gòtic

### Catedral

Pla de la Seu; tel: 93 342 8260; www.catedralbcn.org; Mon–Fri 8am–7.30pm, Sat–Sun 8am–6pm; free except 12.30–5pm daily; metro: Liceu/Jaume I; map p.138 B3

The construction of the cathedral began in 1298 and continued until the mid-15th century, though the neo-Gothic façade was actually not built until the late 19th century.

The main area consists of three naves and an apse with an ambulatory beneath an octagonal dome. Two 14th- and 15th-century towers rise at each end of the transept. Beneath the main altar is the crypt of Santa Eulàlia, and of particular note are the dome's multicoloured keystones.

### THE CLOISTER

On one side is the Santa Eulàlia Portal, which leads to the cathedral cloister, perhaps the most atmospheric part of the cathedral, where the honking of the resident geese competes with the sound of running water from

The 13 geese *(pictured below)* resident in the Catedral are said to symbolise both the age of, and number of tortures inflicted upon, Santa Eulàlia, co-patron saint of Barcelona, when she was killed.

the pretty fountain, and there is a romantic garden of elegant palms, medlars and magnolia trees, all enclosed by the 15th-century wrought-iron railings.

### Sinagoga Mayor

C/Marlet 5; tel: 93 317 0790; www.calldebarcelona.org;

Mon–Fri 11am–6pm, Sun 11am–3pm; admission charge; metro: Jaume I/Liceu; map p.138 B3

This area was the Call, or Jewish quarter, until a wave of anti-Semitic violence killed hundreds and forced survivors to flee or convert to Christianity in the 14th century. This tiny 13th-century synagogue is a reminder of that era.

## Sant Pere and Born

### Santa Maria del Mar

Plaça Santa Maria 1; tel: 93 310 2390; Mon–Sat 9am–1.30pm, 4.30–8pm, Sun 10.30am–1.30pm, 4.30–8pm; free; metro: Jaume I; map p.138 C3

One of the most perfect examples of Catalan Gothic church architecture, with solid and blunt-edged elegance typical of the style. Built in the 14th century, with the collaboration of all the local corporations, it became a symbol of the economic and political power of Catalonia in this period. The interior is breathtaking in its simplicity and elegance. The church is built in what is

**Left and below:** Sant Pau del Camp.

known as the 'salon' design, with three lofty and almost identical naves, which contribute to the sense of space.

## Raval

### Sant Pau del Camp

C/Sant Pau 101–103; tel: 93 441 0001; Tue–Fri 10.30am–1pm, 4.30–8pm, Sat 10.30am–1pm; admission charge; metro: Paral·lel/Liceu; map p.137 E2

Sant Pau del Camp is one of the few examples of Romanesque architecture in the city. The present building dates from the 12th century, but it incorporates elements of an earlier church that was built in 912. Its small cloister, with unusual carvings, is a gem and exquisitely peaceful.

## The Eixample

### Sagrada Família

C/Mallorca 401; tel: 93 207 3031; www.sagradafamilia.org; summer: daily 9am–8pm, winter: daily 9am–6pm; admission charge; metro: Sagrada Família; map p.135 D2

**Right:** detail from the façade of the Sagrada Família.

Gaudí's vast, unfinished temple celebrated Mass in the crypt on 19 March (St Joseph's day) 2007 to celebrate 125 years since construction began. When it will be held in the church proper is anyone's guess. For now this extraordinary building is the city's top tourist attraction, averaging 2.5 million visitors a year.

SEE ALSO MODERNISME, P.83

## Upper Neighbourhoods

### Monestir de Pedralbes

Baixada del Monestir 9, Pedralbes; tel: 93 256 2122; summer: Tue–Sat 10am–5pm, winter: Tue–Sat 10am–2pm, Sun 10am–3pm; admission charge; FGC: Reina Elisenda

The Pedralbes convent was founded in 1326 by Queen Elisenda de Montcada, who herself took the vows of the Order of St Clare. Today some 20 nuns are still in residence. It is best-known for its fine Gothic architecture and unusual three-tiered cloister, while the rooms that are open to the public provide an insight into the day-to-day life of the convent's inhabitants.

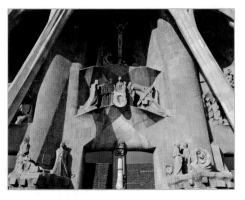

# Essentials

Barcelona is an easily navigated city, and years of tourism have made for an efficient infrastructure for anyone who does not speak the language. In 2007 hundreds of thousands of euros were poured into a scheme to put tourist-oriented signposts on street corners, and in the summer red-jacketed tourist advisers pace the Old City. Tourists even have their own multi-lingual (although it depends who is on duty) police station (La Rambla 76–80; tel: 93 256 2430). For public holidays, *see Festivals, p.48–51*; for information on getting to and around Barcelona, *see Transport, p.126–7*.

## Addresses

Addresses are indicated by street name, number, storey, door. So C/Muntaner, 375, 6° 2a means 375 Muntaner Street, 6th floor, 2nd door. The first floor of a building is known as the *principal*, often abbreviated to pral. Some buildings have an *entresol* between this and the *primera planta*. An *àtic* is a top floor or penthouse, usually with a terrace.

## Consulates

**Australia**
Plaça Gal·la Placídia 1, Gràcia; tel: 93 490 9013; map p.134 B4
**Canada**
C/Elisenda de Pinós 10, Sarrià; tel: 93 204 2700
**Ireland**
Gran Via Carles III, 94, Les Corts; tel: 93 491 5021; map p.132 B4
**United Kingdom**
Avda Diagonal, 477, 13°, Eixample; tel: 93 366 6200; map p.133 E3
**United States**
Passeig Reina Elisenda 23, Sarrià; tel: 93 280 2227

| Metric to Imperial Conversions | |
| --- | --- |
| Metres – Feet 1 | = 3.28 |
| Kilometres – Miles 1 | = 0.62 |
| Hectares – Acres 1 | = 2.47 |
| Kilos – Pounds 1 | = 2.2 |

## Emergencies

**Fire, ambulance** and **police**: dial 112

## Health

EU NATIONALS
Residents of EEA (European Economic Area) countries, which means EU countries

plus Switzerland, Liechtenstein, Iceland and Norway, are entitled to receive state medical treatment in Spain if they have a European Health Insurance Card (EHIC), which must be obtained in their own country. In the UK this can be done online, by phone or by post (www.ehic.org.uk; tel: 0845 606 2030).
**International Association for Medical Assistance to Travellers (IAMAT)**
40 Regal Road, Guelph, Ontario, N1K 1B5, Canada; tel: 519 836 0102; www.iamat.org
This non-profit group offers members fixed rates for medical treatment. Members receive a medical record completed by their doctor and a directory of English-speaking IAMAT doctors who are on call 24 hours a day. Membership is free, but donations are appreciated.

## Money

The currency is the euro (€). Banknotes are issued in 5, 10, 20, 50, 100, 200 and 500; coins in denominations of 1, 2, 5, 10, 20 and 50 céntimos, and €1 and €2.

**Left:** Barcelona is clearly signed and easy to navigate.

Catalunya (look for the giant 'i') is the main city tourist information centre.

**El Prat Airport**
Terminals A and B; tel: 93 478 4704; open daily 9am–9pm

**Ajuntament**
Plaça Sant Jaume, Barri Gòtic; Mon–Fri 9am–8pm, Sat 10am–8pm, Sun 10am–2pm

**Sants Station**
Summer daily 8am–8pm; winter: Mon–Fri 8am–8pm, weekends/holidays 8am–2pm

### Useful Websites

www.barcelonaturisme.com
www.barcelona-metropolitan.com
www.bcn.cat
www.gencat.cat
www.gencat.net/turistex
www.spain.info
www.spaintour.com

### Visas

Passports are required for people of all nationalities entering Spain. Visas are needed by non-EU nationals, unless their country has a reciprocal arrangement with Spain; if in doubt, check with the Spanish Embassy in your home country.

Most banks have cashpoints (ATMs), operating 24 hours a day, where money can be withdrawn using most credit and debit cards.

### Post

Stamps can be bought in the many *estancs* to be found in every district. These are also tobacconists, and are easily recognisable by their orange-and-brown logo, 'Tabac'.

The main post office is at the bottom of Via Laietana near the port, in Plaça Antoni López. It is open Mon–Fri 9am–9pm, Sat 9am–1pm.

### Telephones

Telephone booths are well distributed throughout the city, and many bars also have payphones. Public telephones take all euro coins and most accept credit cards. The minimum charge for a local call is 20 céntimos. Telephone cards are available in *estancs* (tobacconists) and post offices. International reverse-charge (call-collect) calls cannot be made from a phone box. To call Spain, you have to dial: + 34 +city area

Barcelona has a bad reputation for petty crime, and handbags, cameras and even rucksacks are regularly snatched in broad daylight. Wear your handbag across your chest, keep your camera hidden and do not flash your wallet around. Carry enough money for the day, leaving the rest in the safe-deposit box at your hotel.

code +number. The area code for Barcelona is 93.

### Time

Spain is GMT+1 hour (+2 end Mar–end Oct). When it is noon in Barcelona, it is 6am in New York, 10pm in Sydney.

### Tourist Information

For general tourist information about the city, call 010 or 93 285 3834. In addition to the offices below, there are stands in La Rambla, Plaça Espanya and Barceloneta.
**Plaça de Catalunya**
Daily 9am–9pm
Under the Plaça de

**Right:** one of the city's tourist information booths.

# Excursions

Barcelona is one of those uniquely privileged places: not only is it a fantastic city, it is also a geographically brilliant one. Within striking distance are the rugged cliffs and cute fishing villages of the Costa Brava, contrasting with the honey-coloured towns, rolling hills and sunflower fields of the Empordà; the lively resorts of the Costa Dorada and a choice of several distinctive wine regions; the slow-paced market towns of the interior and the rice paddies and water sports of the Ebro Delta. And it's all within reach of the city centre and easily accessible by train, bus or car.

## The Costa Brava

If beaches are your thing they don't come better than the coves that skirt the rugged cliffs of the Costa Brava. Fringed by pine trees with jewel-blue water, it's possible to walk for miles along the coastal path here and discover your own hidden gems.

A good day trip kicks off at **S'Agaro** (accessible by bus from the Estació d'Autobusos Barcelona-Nord). Follow the Camino de Ronda around the cliffs until you get to **Cala de Sa Conca** – a perfect scalloped beach and a good place to stop for lunch – be aware, though, if you opt to continue walking, it's a good hour along the rather grim and built-up front of Platja d'Aro.

The best beaches inevitably are only accessible by road or sea, and if you have a few days it's worth hiring a car to get to them. **Begur**, **Tamariu**, **Llafranc** and **Calella de Palafrugell** are all worth seeking out. Alternatively, take the train to Blanes, where you can hop aboard a small cruiser that drops people up and down the coast. Note that the area is packed during July and August, but the rest of the year – and particularly midweek – it's magically peaceful.

> **Ski days:** Yes, it really is true. Barcelona's nearest ski lift is but two hours away, making a day trip entirely possible. **Vall de Nùria** ski resort (www.vallde nuria.com) is more of an adventure in the sense that you have a take a cog railway from Ribes de Freser (about 1½ hours by train from Barcelona) to get there. There are only 10 runs, but the pistes, surrounded by a sea of jagged peaks, are *Lord of the Rings* material. A little further away, **La Molina** (www.la molina.com) offers a far greater variety of runs, with something to suit all levels and ages. Both have accommodation options. Finally, if you want to try your hand at the latest sport to hit the slopes, snow kiting, contact Iain Hanny at Kite Frenzy (www.kitefrenzy.com), located on the beach in Barceloneta for more information.

## The Costa Dorada

The main draw of the 'gold' coast is the resort town of **Sitges** – a smart, sexy little town with whitewashed houses and plenty of wildlife (*see p.22–3*). But if you're looking for something a little more sedate, continue further south to Vilanova, Tarragona or even l'Ametlla de Mar, which has prettier beaches. All are accessible by train from Sants or Passeig de Gràcia and are good places for catching some rays, especially if you have kids in tow, and scoring a paella on the beach.

From **Vilanova** it's possible to walk back along the cliffs stopping at the beaches en route for a dip (note: they are predominantly gay and nude) all the way to Sitges (about two hours), which is wonderful in spring and autumn. **Tarragona**'s main draw is its impressive Roman ruins – amphitheatre, walls and aqueduct – though the town itself isn't wildly interesting. If you want to treat yourself after absorbing a little ancient history, continue 30

**Left:** the terracotta-toned buildings in Girona.

rewarding for culture vultures: don't miss the Jewish quarter and museum, credited with being the birthplace of Kabbalah, and the cathedral. Girona is also a good base for exploring this lovely region, although the prettiest towns like **Pals** and **Peratallada** are only accessible by car. Both have an extraordinary number of great restaurants for foodies, while nearby **Ullastret** is home to impressive Iberian ruins. Not for nothing is this area known as the 'golden triangle' or the 'Tuscany of Catalonia', and you'll notice plenty of swanky boutiques, gourmet stores and well-heeled Catalans on their summer holidays.

minutes south to **Torredembarra**, home to the fabulously minimalist Hotel Ra (Avda Sanatori 1; tel: 977 694 200; www.hotelra.com) with its super-posh La Prairie Spa.

### The Ebro Delta

Spain's great river is 910km (565 miles) long, flowing all the way from the Picos in Cantabria and finally coming out on the Costa Dorada; for adventure sports enthusiasts it has it all. Where it meets the sea is a hugely popular destination for wind-and-kite surfers, while its lower reaches are its most beautiful and most active for messing about on the water: fishing for catfish or oysters, canoeing, barge-boats (try www.badiatucana.com based in Riba Roja) and bird-watching among them.

It's a relatively undiscovered region and great for travellers looking to get off the beaten path, with several noteworthy places to visit, such as **Miravet**, a hanging village above the banks of the river, as well as wonderful hiking, caving and mountain climbing in the Cardó mountain range.

### The Empordà

**Girona**, the capital of the region, is quickly making a name for itself as a destination in its own right, with a number of boutique hotels, great bars and restaurants opening up. Although definitely more conservative than Barcelona, it has a distinctly upmarket air that appeals to many, and its rich history makes it particularly

### Wine Country

The question perhaps is not what, but where when it comes to making wine your theme. With nine separate regions to choose from, some are better-suited to visitors than others. In the **Penedès**, exploring the cava *bodegas* is the way to go: you can hop on the train to **Sant Sadurni d'Anoia** and Freixenet is literally on the platform. Alternatively, take a cab to **Cordoniu** – a World Heritage Site for its Modernista winery – for a more upmarket bottle of fizz. Serious wine lovers can see more (but taste less) if they hire a car and hit the country solo. Friendly options for visitors are **Albet I Noya** (www.albetinoya.com), **Jean Leon** (www.jeanleon.com) and **Torres** (www.torres.es).
SEE ALSO FOOD AND DRINK, P.55–6

**Left:** Freixenet's well-stocked wine cellar.

# Fashion

The fact that Barcelona is better-known as the biannual host of the influential Bread and Butter streetwear trade show than for the *Pasarela Gaudí* (fashion week) says a lot about the way it dresses. It may not have the big-name designers of Paris, New York or London, but a new wave of young, home-grown talent is increasingly turning heads. While the city maintains its laissez-faire outlook – you'll rarely be asked to wear a tie in any restaurant, for example, but don't expect to hit the clubs in trainers – its place as one of the most fashionable destinations in Europe has seen the same effervescent energy emerge on the catwalks.

## Barcelona Designers and Boutiques

### Custo
Plaça de les Olles 7, Born; tel: 93 268 7893; www.custo-barcelona.com; Mon–Sat 10am–10pm, metro: Jaume I; map p.138 C2

Firmly established at the top of Barcelona's fashion hierarchy, the Dalmau brothers' brand is defined by the colourful scenes depicted on the garments. They mix crochet with cotton, knitwear with patchwork, cotton with lace, creating a boho look inspired by their years in California.

### El Delgado Buil
C/Lledó 4–6, Barri Gòtic; tel: 93 315 2073; www.eldelgado buil.com; Mon–Sat 11am–2pm,

4–8pm; metro: Jaume I; map p.138 B3

They made the headlines a couple of years ago with their revolutionary 'unisex' concept, and since then there's been no stopping them. Think eccentric fringed shirts, balloon dresses and drawn-on faces, mainly on white.

### Fresh from the Lab
C/Enric Granados 94, Eixample; tel: 93 218 0404; www.fresh fromthelab.com; Mon–Fri 10.30am–2.30pm, 5–8.30pm, Sat 11.30am–2.30pm; metro: Universitat; map p.134 A3

Inspired by architecture, design, art and sculpture, 20 international artists and designers got together to create this unique line of highly covetable t-shirts.

### Lois Jeans
C/Bonaire 2, Born; tel: 93 310 6498; www.loisjeans.com; Mon–Sat 11am–9pm; metro: Barceloneta or Jaume I; map p.138 C2

With their prancing bull logo, these emblematic jeans were a symbol of the seventies. Famed for their flares, they remain among the most covetable brands around.

### Loisaidabcn (Lower East Side)
C/Flassaders 42; tel: 93 295 5492; www.loisaidabcn.com; Mon–Sat 11am–9pm; metro: Barceloneta or Jaume I; map p.138 C3

One of the best concept shops in town, with a wide range of less known brands and recycled vintage (it's a good place to pick up a faux fur, for example). Into the mix go household antiques, furniture, records, posters and curios like cameras and pipes.

## High-Street Tigers

### Armand Basi
Passeig de Gràcia 49, Eixample; tel: 93 215 1421; www.armand basi.com; Mon–Sat 10am–9pm; metro: Passeig de Gràcia; map p.134 B2

A classic for tailored men's and women's wear, Basi's distinctive Mediterranean styling has been going strong for over two decades now. Perfect for updating a jaded work wardrobe.

### Blanco
C/Pelai 1, Eixample; tel: 93 318 2340; Mon–Sat 10am–9pm;

> **The rag district:** The city's hottest designers and most happening boutiques are clustered together in a small corner of the Born. This bijou 'rag district' occupies several blocks between the Avda Marquès de l'Argentera to the south, C/Comerç to the east, C/Princesa to the north and C/Argenteria to the west.

**Left:** Custo's bright prints.

**Size conversions**
**Women:** 36 (UK 8, US 6);
38 (UK 10, US 8); 40 (UK 12, US
10); 42 (UK 14, US 12); 44 (UK
16, US 14); 46 (UK 18, US 16).
**Men:** 87 (UK/US 34); 91 (UK/US
36); 97 (UK/US 38); 102 (UK/US
40); 107 (UK/US 42); 112
(UK/US 44); 117 (UK/US 46).

metro: Catalunya; map p.134 A1
This is cheap, cheerful
fashion that almost defies the
need to pack anything at all.
Particularly strong on
seasonal themes: hip coats
for autumn and winter,
sparkly party dresses and
summer frocks.

### Desigual
C/Argenteria 65, Born; no
phone; www.desigual.com;
Mon–Sat 10am–9pm; metro:
Jaume 1; map p.138 B3
Brash and bold Desigual now
has something like 3,000
stores around the world and
counting. Think off-the-wall
looks, buckets of colour and
rule-breaking tailoring.

### Mango
Passeig de Gràcia 65, Eixample;
tel: 93 215 7530; www.mango.es;
Mon–Sat 10am–9pm; metro:
Passeig de Gràcia; map p.134 B2
Are you team Mango, or
team Zara? Probably both
when the price is right.
Mango is unbeatable for staples like trouser suits, pencil
skirts, stretch long-sleeved t-
shirts and perky jackets.

### Zara
Portal de l'Àngel 32–34, Barri
Gòtic; tel: 93 301 0898; www.
zara.com; Mon–Sat 10am–9pm;
metro: Catalunya; map p.138 B4
A great all-rounder covering
men, women and children as
well as home wares. The quality's good, and it's unfailingly
on-trend with collections
updated every few weeks.

## Menswear

### El Ganso
C/Bonaire 6, Born; tel: 93 268
9257; www.elganso.com;
Mon–Sat 11am–9pm; metro:
Barceloneta or Jaume I; map

p.138 C2
Think unusual wardrobe classics rather than fickle fashion
at this exclusive menswear
boutique. The range includes
smart tweed jackets ranging
from herringbone to tartan,
colourful polo shirts, preppy
ties and baseball boots.

### M69
C/Rec 28, Born; tel: 93 310
4236; www.m69barcelona.com;
Mon–Sat 11am–9pm; metro:
Jaume I or Barceloneta; map
p.138 C3
Fully stocked with the season's most covetable lines,
including exclusive Spanish
rights to Helmut Lang. Slick
presentation ups the experience to shopping nirvana.

### Special Events Man
C/Vigatans 11, Born; tel: 93 268
8738; www.joanestrada.com;
Mon 5–9pm, Tue–Fri 10.30am–
9pm, Sat 11am–9pm; metro:
Jaume I; map p.138 B3

**Right:** branded denim and
B-movie t-shirts at Lois.

It's not the cleverest name on earth, but it's a great place to pick up a party outfit or even a wedding tux. Everyone from Hugo Boss to Plata de Palo is represented; all you'll need is your credit card.

### Womenswear

**Comité**
C/Notariat 8, Raval; tel: 93 317 6883; www.comite

barcelona.com; Mon–Sat noon–8.30pm; metro: Sant Antoni or Liceu; map p.138 A4
A great example of the co-operative mentality so strong in Barcelona, this store is shared by seven young designers, each with a unique perspective. The range is fun, frivolous and a little bit cheeky.

**MTX**
C/Rec 32; tel: 93 319 1398; www.mertxe-hernandez.com; Mon–Sun 5–9pm, Tue–Sat noon–2pm, 5–9pm; metro: Barceloneta or Jaume I; map p.138 C3
One of the rising stars of the Catalan fashion designer circuit, Mertxe makes quirky hand-printed t-shirts, unusual cocktail dresses and coats of many colours.

**Tomates Fritos**
C/Laforja 94; tel: 93 209 3979; www.tomatesfritos.com; Mon–Sat noon–9pm; metro: Barceloneta or Jaume I; map p.133 E4
Teeny tiny Tomates Fritos packs a whole lot of style into a small space by only stocking one or two of everything. Beautifully tailored coats and jackets, feather-light tops, silk shirts and skirts bring effortless elegance to a working gal's wardrobe.

LINGERIE
**Le Boudoir**
C/Canuda 21, Barri Gòtic; tel: 93 302 5281; www.leboudoir.net; Mon–Fri 10am–8.30pm, Sat 10am–9pm; metro: Catalunya; map p.138 B4
The sexiest underwear shop in town works hard to titillate the casual browser. Luxury bras and knickers are interspersed with fluffy handcuffs, velvet ticklers and designer sex toys.

**Women's Secret**
C/Portaferrissa 7–9, Barri Gòtic; tel: 93 318 9242; www.women secret.com; Mon–Sat 10am–9pm; metro: Liceu; map p.138 B3
Practical pants, PJs and bed socks in bright colours and funky patterns, this highly successful chain is aimed at gals who opt for comfort over corsetry.

SHOES AND ACCESSORIES
**Beatriz Furest**
C/Esparteria 1, Born; tel: 93 268

**Left:** Le Boudoir.

metal mesh ties, belts and bags have garnered an international following.

### Hatquarters
Plaça de la Llana 6, La Ribera; tel: 93 310 1802; Mon–Sat 11am–2pm, 5–8pm; metro: Jaume I; map p.138 B3
This narrow shop with bow-beamed ceilings uses its red-brick walls to display an extraordinary collection of hats. From a Britney-type trilby to a harlequin peaked cap, they've got you covered.

### Vialis
C/Vidrieria 15, Born; tel: 93 319 9491; Mon–Sat 10am–10pm; metro: Jaume I or Barceloneta; map p.138 C2
The unique styling, divine comfort and good looks of Vialis's shoe collection make this a must for shoe obsessives. Their past years' four-inch clog boots were a contemporary classic; pop in to see what's big this year.

3796; www.beatrizfurest.com; Mon–Sat 11am–3pm, 4–8.30pm; metro: Jaume I or Barceloneta; map p.138 C2
Unique bags and purses in butter-soft leather with rich colours and finishes. The clutches are particularly desirable. Walk in for one, walk out with two or three.

### Blow
C/Doctor Dou 11, Raval; tel: 93 302 3698; www.leswingvintage.com; Mon–Fri 10.30am–2.30pm, 4.30–8.30pm; metro: Sant Antoni or Liceu; map p.138 A4
Upmarket vintage shoes and accessories in a fabulously retro setting. Rare finds include YSL sunglasses and Chanel handbags, platform shoes from the 1970s and larger-than-life costume jewellery.

### Camper
Plaça del Àngels 6, Raval; tel: 93 302 4124; www.camper.com; Mon–Sat 10am–10pm; metro: Sant Antoni or Liceu; map p.138 A4
If you're a fan of sensible shoes with a twist then

Camper is an absolute must. The Mallorcan label is cheaper here than in Northern Europe, and the injection of ideas from designer Jaime Hayon have turned the collection from geeky to glam overnight.

### Castañer
C/Mestre Nicolau 23, Sarrià; tel: 93 414 2428; www.castaner.com; Mon–Sat 10.30am–8.15pm; FCG: La Bonanova; map p.133 E4
Home of the original wedge-heel espadrille designed by Lorenzo Castañer for Yves Saint Laurent in the 1960s. Copies abound, but the real deal is a summer must-have for style seekers: cool, comfortable and classy, they come in all the colours of the rainbow and a multitude of styles.

### Comtessa Nº Uno
C/Comtessa de Sobradiel 1, Born; tel: 93 317 8756; Mon–Fri 11am–2pm, 4–8pm, Sat until 8.30pm; metro: Jaume I; map p.138 B3
Jewellery designer Laura B shows a collection twice a year as well as producing one-offs. Her trademark

**Vintage spoils:** Little C/Riera Baixa in the Raval is dedicated to high-end vintage and second-hand stores. These range from military wear to old costumes from the Liceu, some dating as far back as the 17th century.

# Festivals

It is almost impossible to pass through Barcelona and not coincide with one festival or another; here we've listed just a selection, but it is always worth checking the Ajuntament's website, www.bcn.cat/agenda. Certain themes run through most of the city's festivals, particularly each neighbourhood's *festa major*. You can expect to see towering papier-mâché giants and dragons, a display of *castellers* (human towers) and *sardanes* (the traditional Catalan dance) in public squares. These are often taken over by rock or jazz bands at night, and the bigger festivals will often include fireworks on the beach.

## Public Holidays

**1 Jan**, Cap d'Any; **6 Jan**, Reis; **Good Friday**, Divendres Sant; **Easter Monday**, Dilluns de Pasqua Florida; **1 May**, Festa del Treball; **Whitsun Mon**, Dilluns de Pasqua Granada; **24 June**, Sant Joan; **15 Aug**, L'Assumpció; **11 Sept**, Diada Nacional; **24 Sept**, La Mercè; **1 Nov**, Tots Sants; **6 Dec**, Dia de la Constitució; **8 Dec**, La Immaculada; **25 Dec**, Nadal; **26 Dec**, Sant Esteve.

## Festivals and Events

### JANUARY

**Dia dels Reis**
5 Jan; various venues; www.bcn.cat/nadal
Parade of the Three Kings to celebrate epiphany.

**Festa dels Tres Tombs**
17 Jan; Sant Antoni market to La Rambla; www.xarxantoni.net
Parade of horses and carriages to mark St Anthony's day.

### FEBRUARY

**Carnaval (Carnival)**
Week of Shrove Tuesday; various venues; www.bcn.cat/carnaval
Neighbourhood parades and open-air concerts.

**Santa Eulàlia**
Week of 12 Feb; all over Barcelona; www.bcn.cat/santaeulalia
Children's festival with street parties and activities.

**Festival Internacional de Percussió**
Mid-Feb; L'Auditori, C/Lepant 150, Eixample; tel: 93 247 9300; www.auditori.org
International percussion festival.

### MARCH

**Marató Barcelona**
Early Mar; around the city from Plaça Espanya; tel: 902 43 1763; www.maratobarcelona.com
City marathon.

**Festes de Sant Medir**
Week of 3 Mar; Gràcia; tel: 93 285 0670; www.santmedir.org
The crowds are showered with sweets thrown from horseback and carts.

---

The must-have item for shoppers at the Santa Llúcia Christmas fair is the *caganer* ('crapper'). This little squatting man, with his trousers round his ankles, is considered a lucky addition to every home's Nativity scene.

**Left:** festival lanterns light up the streets.

**Left:** the Three Wise Kings in a poster for Nadal (26 Dec).

www.auditori.org
Month-long medieval music festival.

**Dia del Treball (May Day)**
1 May; various venues
Day of marches and protests led by the trade unions.

**Festival Internacional de Poesia**
Early May; various venues; www.bcn.cat/barcelonapoesia
Poetry festival.

**La Cursa del Corte Inglés**
Early May; across Barcelona; www.elcorteingles.com
Seven-mile (10-km) race round the city.

**Sant Ponç**
11 May; C/Hospital, Raval and other venues; www.bcn.cat
Stalls selling herbs, cheese and honey to celebrate the patron saint of herbalists.

**Dia Internacional dels Museus (International Museum Day)**
18 May; various venues; http://icom.museum/imd.html
The municipal museums are free and hold special events.

**Festival de Flamenco de Ciutat Vella**
End May; CCCB, C/Montalegre 5, Raval and various venues; tel: 93 306 4100; www.tallerde musics.com
Old City Flamenco Festival.

**La Tamborinada**
End May; Parc de la Ciutadella,

**El Feile**
Week of 17 Mar; various venues; www.elfeile.com
Festival of Irish and Celtic culture coinciding with St Patrick's Day.

**Diumenge de Rams**
Palm Sunday; cathedral; www.bcn.cat
The Blessing of the Palms is followed by a parade and a small street fair.

APRIL
**Festival Guitarra**
Apr–June; various venues; tel: 93 481 7040; www.theproject.es
Guitar festival.

**Sant Jordi**
23 April; various venues; www.bcn.cat
Feast day of Sant Jordi (St George), the patron saint of Catalonia. Couples exchange gifts of red roses and books.

**BAFF**
End Apr–early May; various venues; www.baff-bcn.org

**Right:** an exhibit during the visiting Cow Parade festival; the BAFF is a city stalwart.

Barcelona Asian Film Festival.

**Dia de la Terra**
Late Apr; Passeig Lluis Companys and Parc de la Ciutadella, Born; www.diadelaterra.org
Two-day festival of the environment.

**Feria de Abril**
Late Apr–early May; Parc del Fòrum; www.fecac.com
A snapshot of Andalusian culture, with flamenco shows in marquees and every sort of fried fish imaginable.

MAY
**Festival de Música Antiga**
Apr–May; L'Auditori, C/Lepant 150, Eixample; tel: 93 247 9300;

Born; www.fundaciolaroda.net
Children's festival of concerts
and circus performances.

**Festa dels Cors de la Barceloneta**
Whitsun; around Barceloneta;
www.bcn.es
Neighbourhood festival, with
fancy-dress parades and outdoor concerts.

**Primavera Sound**
End May; Parc de la Fòrum;
www.primaverasound.com
Three days of indie bands
and films.

**L'Ou com Balla**
Corpus Christi; cathedral
cloisters and other venues;
www.bcn.cat
Decorated fountains sport
the 'dancing egg' on a spout
of water.

JUNE
**De Cajón**
June–July; various venues;
www.theproject.es
Flamenco festival.

**Marató de l'Espectacle**
Early June; Mercat de les Flors,

Plaça Margarida Xirgú, C/Lleida
59; tel: 93 268 1868;
www.marato.com
Two days of non-stop theatri-
cal, circus and comedy performances.

**Sónar Advanced Music Festival**
Mid-June; various venues;
www.sonar.es
World-famous festival of
electronic music.

**Festa de la Música**
21 June; across Barcelona;
www.bcn.cat/festadelamusica
International free music festival, with dozens of open-air
concerts.

**Festival del Grec**
June–Aug; various venues;
www.bcn.cat/grec
Summer festival of theatre,
music and dance.

**Festival de Música Creativa i Jazz de Ciutat Vella**
End June; various venues; tel:
972 864 561; www.bcn.cat
Small venues and bars around
the old city host live jazz.

Left: a *casteller* in action.

**Sant Joan**
23 June; all over Barcelona
The big party of the summer,
with bonfires and fireworks
across town.

JULY
**B-estival**
July; Poble Espanyol, Avda
Marqués de Comillas, Montjuïc;
tel: 93 325 7866; www.b-estival.
com
Festival of mainly African and
Brazilian names, along with
soul and R&B acts.

**Dies de Dansa**
End June–early July; various
venues; www.marato.com
Four days of free outdoor
dance performances.

**Festa Major del Raval**
Mid-July; Raval;
www.ravalnet.org
Three days of concerts and
parades around the Raval
neighbourhood.

**Clàssics als Parcs**
July; various parks;
www.bcn.es/parcsijardin
Night-time classical concerts
throughout the month.

**Summercase**
Mid-July; Parc del Fòrum;
www.summercase.com
Mainstream and indie music
festival over two days.

**Mas i Mas Festival**
Late July–early Sept; various
venues; www.masimas.com
Jazz and Latin music festival.

AUGUST
**Nits d'Estiu**
Every Wed in Aug; CaixaForum,
Casaramona, Avda Marquès de
Comillas 6–8, Montjuïc; tel: 93
476 8600;
www.fundacio.lacaixa.es
Late nights at the Caixa-
Forum gallery, with concerts
and films.

**Jazz a Ciutadella**
Wed and Fri; Parc de la Ciutadella, Born; www.bcn.es/
parcsijardins

From 6.30–8.30pm on Saturdays and noon–2pm on Sundays, locals join hands to dance the peculiarly sedate *sardana* in front of the Catedral. They are accompanied by bands playing *cobles*, oddly composed and slightly reedy numbers.

Free outdoor jazz shows at the bandstand.

**Gandules**
Tue, Wed, Thur; CCCB, C/Montalegre 5, Raval; tel: 93 306 4100; www.cccb.org
Outdoor free cinema screenings.

**Festa de Sant Roc**
Week of 16 Aug; Barri Gòtic; www.bcn.es
The patron saint of the Barri Gòtic is celebrated with parties, activities and fireworks.

**Festa Major de Gràcia**
Late Aug; Gràcia; www.festamajordegracia.org
The best of all the *festes majors*, famous for its street decorations.

**Festa Major de Sants**
Late Aug; Sants; www.festamajordesants.org
Parties and fireworks for the Sants neighbourhood bash.

SEPTEMBER
**Festival L'Hora del Jazz**
Sept; various venues; www.amjm.org
Low-key jazz festival, with many free concerts.

**Diada Nacional**
11 Sept; across Barcelona
Emotions run high on Catalan National Day, with marches and demonstrations.

**Festival Asia**
Mid-Sept; various venues; tel: 93 368 0836; www.casaasia.es/festival
Films, music and culture from all over Asia.

**Weekend Dance**
Mid-Sept; Parc del Fòrum; www.weekendance.es
One day dance-music festival.

**Barcelona Acció Musical (BAM)**
Week of 24 Sept; various venues; www.bam.es
Programme of concerts run in conjunction with the Mercè celebrations.

**Festes de la Mercè**
Week of 24 Sept; across Barcelona; www.bcn.cat/merce
Huge celebrations over several days to celebrate Barcelona's patron saint.

**Festa Major de la Barceloneta**
End Sept; Barceloneta; www.cascantic.net
Neighbourhood festival with parades and concerts.

OCTOBER
**LEM Festival**
Oct; various venues, Gràcia; tel: 93 237 3737; www.graciaterritori.com
Festival of experimental music.

**Festival de Tardor Ribermúsica**
Late Oct; various venues, Born; tel: 93 319 3089; www.ribermusica.org
Dozens of small, free concerts in all sorts of venues throughout the Born.

**Festival de Opera Butxaca**
End Oct–early Dec; various venues; tel: 93 301 8485; www.festivaloperabutxaca.org
Festival of new and pocket opera.

**La Castanyada**
31 Oct–1 Nov; Montjuïc cemetery and across Barcelona
Gravestones are decorated and chestnuts are roasted for All Saints' Day.

NOVEMBER
**Wintercase Barcelona**
Nov; Sala Razzmatazz 1, C/Almogàvers 122, Poblenou; tel: 93 320 82 00; www.wintercase.com
Indie music festival.

**Festival Internacional de Jazz de Barcelona**
Nov/Dec; various venues; www.theproject.es
Big names from around the world.

DECEMBER
**Fira de Sant Eloi**
1–24 Dec; C/Argenteria, Born; www.bcn.cat/agenda
Street fair with handmade Christmas gifts and live music.

**Fira de Santa Llúcia**
1–24 Dec; cathedral; www.bcn.es/nadal
Another Christmas street fair, this one filling the area around the cathedral.

**Drap Art**
Mid-Dec; CCCB, C/Montalegre 5, Raval; www.drapart.org
An improbably good three-day recycling festival. It includes live music and dance as well as workshops and a fair.

**Día dels Inocents**
28 Dec; all over Barcelona
Catalunya's answer to April Fool's Day. Traditionally, paper cut-out figures are stuck to victims' backs.

**Cap d'Any (New Year's Eve)**
31 Dec
The biggest gathering is in Plaça Catalunya, where people eat one grape with each chime of midnight.

**Left:** Smashing Pumpkins performing at Summercase.

# Film

Since Salvador Dalí and Luís Buñuel wrote, directed and starred in *Un Chien Andalou* in 1929, Spanish cinema has had an impact and verve seemingly out of all proportion to the size of its output. Spaniards are keen filmgoers, and the popularity of cities such as Barcelona and Madrid as filmsets serves as a constant reminder of the production process. The Catalan capital was smeared with mud for Tom Twyker's *Perfume*, and in 2007 Woody Allen, Scarlett Johansson and Javier Bardem descended on the city to film Allen's *Vicky Cristina Barcelona*, to be released in late 2008 and described as his 'love letter' to the city.

## Spanish Cinema

The undisputed king of Spanish cinema since the 1980s has been **Pedro Almodóvar**, but other modern directors with celebrated auteur status include **Julio Medem** (*Cows, Lovers of the Arctic Circle, Sex and Lucía, The Basque Ball*); **Alejandro Amenábar** (*Open Your Eyes, The Sea Inside*), and **Bigas Luna** (*Jamón, Jamón*). Recently many directors have been increasing their potential audiences by making films in English and using internationally known actors, a trend that became popular

after Amenábar cast Nicole Kidman in *The Others* and produced it in English. Catalan director Isabel Coixet has

worked with Sarah Polley, Tim Robbins and Amanda Plummer in films such as *My Life Without Me* and *The Secret Life of Words*, and more recently Álex de la Iglesia directed Elijah Wood and John Hurt in *The Oxford Murders*.

## Festivals

The grandest of the many film festivals in Catalunya is the **Festival Internacional de Cinema de Catalunya**, held every October in Sitges. Officially it's a showcase for 'fantasy' films, but the label is used loosely and includes some mainstream Hollywood fare. (See www.cinemasitges.com.)

In Barcelona itself there's a panoply of small independent festivals, many of them centred on the **CCCB**. (See www.cccb.org and www.bcn.cat/agenda for more information.)
SEE ALSO MUSEUMS AND GALLERIES, P.86–7

## Cinemas

All the cinemas below show films in their original language

**Left:** the Teatre Coliseum on Gran Vía Corts shows films.

**Left:** Javier Bardem in *No Country for Old Men.*

### IMAX Port Vell

Moll d'Espanya, Port Vell; tel: 93 225 1111; www.imaxportvell. com; metro: Barceloneta or Drassanes; map p.138 B1

The city's only IMAX cinema is quite an experience, but tends to run the usual gamut of short nature and planetary films, around half of them in 3D and some in OMNIMAX.

### Méliès Cinemes

C/Villarroel 102, Eixample; tel: 93 451 0051; www.cines melies.net; metro: Urgell; map p.133 E1

The Méliès has a similar mission to the Filmoteca, *left*, with a mix of loved classics and auteur cinema. Tickets are equally cheap, with books of 10 for €20.

### Renoir-Floridablanca

C/Floridablanca 135, Eixample; tel: 93 228 9393; www.cines renoir.com; metro: Sant Antoni; map p.137 E4

A good mix of accessible and quirky independent films, in a comfortable, four-screen setting.

### Verdi

C/Verdi 32, Gràcia; tel: 93 238 7990; www.cines-verdi.com; metro: Fontana; map p.134 C4

A impressive range of independent and world cinema attracts a mostly young crowd to this and the Verdi Park around the corner (C/Torrijos 49). Queues are long.

### Yelmo Icària Cineplex

C/Salvador Espriú 61, Vila Olímpica; tel: 93 221 7585/902 22 0922; www.yelmocineplex.es; metro: Ciutadella-Vila Olímpica; map p.139 E2

A huge multiplex showing Hollywood blockbusters and other mainstream fodder.

At the 2008 Academy Awards ceremony, Javier Bardem became the first ever Spanish actor to win an Oscar, for his performance in the Coen brothers' *No Country For Old Men.*

(listed in newspapers as 'VO', or *versión original*), with subtitles in Spanish or, occasionally, Catalan.

### Casablanca Gràcia

C/de Girona 173–175, Eixample; tel: 93 459 0326; metro: Diagonal or Verdaguer; map p.134 C3

The newest addition to the VO scene in Barcelona, with six screens showing Spanish and international, mostly independent, films.

### Cine Coliseum

Gran Via de les Corts Catalanes 595; www.grupbalana.com; tel: 90 242 4243; metro: Passeig de Gràcia; map p.134 B4

A historic, single-screen cinema. The Coliseum occasionally puts on live performances as well as films.

### Cine Maldà

C/Pi 5, Barri Gòtic; tel: 93 481 3704; www.cinemalda.com; metro: Catalunya or Liceu; map p.138 B3

These days the tiny Maldà functions mainly as a Bollywood cinema, but also shows a handful of decent independent films. On Tuesday nights it's taken over by Cine Ambigú, who put on European art-house movies.

### Filmoteca de la Generalitat

Avda Sarrià 31–33, Eixample; tel: 93 410 7590; www.gencat.cat/cultura/icic/ filmoteca; metro: Hospital Clínic; map p.133 D3

A rep cinema run by the Generalitat and offering cycles of filmic fare at very low prices.

**Left:** a still from a recent film installation at the CCCB.

53

# Food and Drink

It's long been known that Barcelona ranks as one of Europe's top food destinations, in some cases even surpassing them when it comes to culinary ingenuity. Home to a multitude of known and rising stars – among them Ferran Adrìa, Sergi Arola, Carles Abellan and Carme Ruscalleda – it's also a haven of small bistros and hidden gems that are well worth seeking out. The secret is in the produce. Barcelona is blessed in the bounty of the sea, mountains and fertile lands resulting in a cuisine that is as varied and awe-inspiring as its terrain. *See also Bars and Cafés, p.28–35; Restaurants, p.104–13, and Tapas Bars, p.120–23*

### Nature's Bounty and a Bountiful Imagination

Like most Mediterranean countries the focus in Catalonia is on fresh, seasonal products generally cooked without too much fuss or embellishment. As Ferran Adria himself says: no lobster can compare to a perfectly ripe, locally grown tomato. As such, much of the cuisine is based around nuts, garlic, olive oil, tomatoes, herbs and dried fruit that are abundant in the region, with four key sauces providing the substance of many of Catalonia's traditional dishes: *picada* (ground nuts for thickening), *sofrito* (a rich, slowly cooked onion base), *alioli* (garlic and oil for dipping), and *romesco* (peppers and nuts, also for dipping).

Beyond this, Catalan cooks traditionally dance to the beat of their own drum. It is not unusual to see products of the sea combined with those of the land in a style known as *mar i*

muntanya (sea and mountain) such as *mandoguiles amb sepia* (meatballs with cuttlefish), or *gambes amb pollastre* (prawns with chicken).

And yet they are also deeply proud of their more simple pleasures: *pa amb*

tomàquet* – coarse country bread rubbed with a ripe tomato, garlic and drizzled with olive oil forming the basis of many a long, lazy lunch. Topped with anchovies (from L'Escala of course), or local cured sausages from Vic, or goat's and sheep's

**Right:** fresh fruit at La Boqueria and simple squid and chips.

**Left:** wafer-thin Iberian ham carved from the joint.

**Top 5 Seasonal Treats Bolets:** *ceps, rovellons, trompetas del mort,* to name just three, are a must for **fungi** addicts: all wildly delicious and at their peak from October to January. **Castanyes i panellets:** November sees rustic carts take to the streets serving paper cones of freshly roasted chestnuts, while the bakeries offer sweet marzipan cakes rolled in anything from pine nuts to coconut. **Fesols del Ganxet:** big and creamy butter beans, these highly revered pulses come into season in mid-November and are traditionally stewed with clams. **Torró:** a sweetmeat traditionally made using ground almonds and honey, Catalans eat most of theirs at Christmas time. **La gran festa del cava:** a three-day festival takes place every year at the start of October in the cava capital of Sant Sadurni d'Anoia to celebrate the harvest. It's a fun, well-lubricated affair where copious amounts of bubbly are offered by the region's *bodegas* for revelling masses.

cheeses from the mountains, and a handful of small, earthy arbequina olives, a simple picnic lunch quickly becomes a feast for a king.

## Top 10 Catalan Classics

*Arròs Negre* similar to paella, this rib-sticking Sunday lunch uses squid ink to colour and flavour a rice stuffed with clams and cuttlefish.

*Escalivada* grilled peppers, aubergines and sometimes onions, skinned, left to cool and doused in fruity olive oil.

*Esqueixada* a hearty salad of raw shredded salt cod, onions, peppers and olives.

*Espinacs a la Catalana* a popular side-dish of spinach sautéed with pine nuts and raisins.

*Faves a la Catalana* baby broad beans stewed with *botifarra negra* (blood sausage).

*Fideuà* a popular alternative to paella using thin pasta instead and flavoured with seafood – most typically prawns, cuttlefish and clams.

*Oca amb naps* succulent, slowly roasted goose with turnips.

*Suquet* a rich seafood and fish stew similar to the French bouillabaisse.

*Crema Catalana* the ubiquitous Catalan pud of sweet vanilla-scented custard with a burnt-sugar crust.

*Mel I mató* fresh creamy goat's cheese (traditionally wrapped in muslin) and drizzled with runny honey.

## Wine Wonderland

Wine flows faster than water in this town, and for lovers of the vine there's no better place to get to grips with the Catalan DOs *(denominació d'Origen)*. Although dedicated wine bars are still something of a rarity (with the exception of La Vinya del Senyor, see p.30), most places offer a reasonable selection of bottles from the nine local wine-growing areas.

Largely what to buy depends on what you like, but you don't have to spend a vast amount of money to drink well in Barcelona. The price-quality ratio of wine is generally much higher than that in France or Italy. Even young house wines and

those straight from the barrel at more basic tapas bars can be perfectly drinkable if a little rough around the edges. You can always do as locals do and order a bottle of *gaseosa* (sweet soda water) to tame it down.

**WINE GUIDE**
**Alella**
A mere 20 minutes from the city, this coastal region produces lovely fresh white wines. Try the **Marqués de Alella Pansa Blanca** with seafood and fish.
**Conca de Barberà**
A hilly region within sight of

55

the Mediterranean and famous for its Ruta del Cister – a trail of monasteries – as well as its white wines. Cellar Mas Forester is a reliable label to look out for.

### Costers del Segre
Fruit-forward reds are the hallmark of this region. Castell del Remei Gotim Bru never fails as a crowd pleaser.

### Empordà-Costa Brava
Traditionally known for its sweet red garnacha wine, the arrival of young wine-makers here has turned attention to making unusual reds. Vi Novell d'Empordà is similar to Beaujolais Nouveau in style but tricky to get outside of the region. Otherwise look for anything by Oliver Conti.

### Penedès
best known for its cava, the region also boasts a handful of superb wineries making top-flight still wines. Try the organic Chardonnay from Albet I Noya (Spain's first 100% organic winery), juicy Pinot Noir from Can Rafols dels Caus, and the Terrasola range from Jean Leon, which blends big-name varieties with lesser-known local grapes.

### Plá de Bagès
a small region specialising in endemic varieties such as Abadall's Picapoll (a fruity white with plenty of zing).

### Priorato
The king of all the regions – and indeed of much of Spain – Clos de l'Obac makes impressive boutique wines such as the divine white Kyrie, a majestic red Mis-

#### Eating Hours
For breakfast most city dwellers are happy with a croissant and a *tallat* (shot of expresso topped up with hot milk) or a *café amb let* (milky) to get themselves going, though some jolly things along with a shot of brandy or anis too. By 1pm people are getting ready for lunch, perhaps with a small glass of *vermut* (vermouth) over ice and a slice of orange and a couple of anchovies. Nobody sits down to eat until 1.30pm, and generally it's a long, drawn-out affair lasting until about 4pm. If you're on a budget, do as locals do by taking a three-course *menú del dia* as your main meal. At value-packed prices from 8–15 euros they range from reasonable to excellent. Come 9pm folks again start turning their attention to food, typically making reservations for around 9.30–10pm. Catalans like their table linen and liveried service, but if you hanker after something light Barcelona's increasingly becoming a top-spot to *tapear* (tapas-hop) too (see *Tapas Bars, p.120–23*).

erere, and the Moorish sweet wine dolç l'Obac.

### Tarragona
Famed worldwide for its altar wines (still widely exported), stylistically the wines now cater to a wider audience. The sub-region of Montsant (sometimes known as Priorato's poorer cousin since it makes similar-quality wines at a fraction of the price) is the name to look out for, particularly Ètim and kosher wines from the Capçanes winery.

### Terra Alta
The beautiful rolling country-side and Modernista wineries designed by César Martinell make this prime, if relatively unknown touring country. Check out El Pinell de Brai and Gandesa.

### A Guide to Snacking
These days menus at bigger places come in Catalan, Spanish and English, or there's usually someone who can guide you. Smaller tapas bars may offer no menu at all, and you simply point to what you want. Otherwise the following should help in a pinch.
*Albóndigas* meatballs
*Bunyols de bacallà* salt cod fritters
*Cabrales* a potent blue cheese from Asturias
*Calamares a la brasa* grilled whole squid/fried squid rings

*Carxofes* artichokes
*Croquetas* croquettes flavoured with *jamón* (ham) or chicken
*Ensaladilla rusa* a salad of diced veg and potatoes slathered in mayo
*Formatge* cheese
*Gambes* prawns
*Llonganissa* spicy cured sausage
*Fuet* whip-thin cured sausage
*Pa amb tomàquet* bread rubbed with tomato, garlic and olive oil
*Patates allioli* fried potatoes with garlic mayo
*Patates braves* fried potatoes with hot sauce
*Pebrots de Padró* fried green peppers
*Pescaditos* little fried fishes
*Truita* Spanish omelette (can also mean trout)

## Shopping Guide

Do not save your shopping until Monday. You'll find most of the specialist stores are closed.

### Cacao Sampaka
C/Consell de Cent 292, Eixample; tel: 93 272 0833; www.cacaosampaka.com; Mon–Sat 9am–9.30pm; metro: Passeig de Gràcia; map p.134 B2
Not to be missed for chocoholics, this uber-modern store is the brainchild of Albert Adrià (pastry chef at El Bulli and Ferran's younger brother). Specialities include

anchovy and olive chocs, though you can pick up something more pedestrian – including single-estate chocolates – if you wish.

### Casa Gispert
C/Sombrerers 23, Born; tel: 93 319 7535; www.casagispert.com; Tue–Sat 10am–2pm, 5–8pm; metro: Jaume I; map p.138 C3
The old-world home of superlative dried nuts and fruit, freshly roasted coffee, teas and ready-made packs of wild mushroom risotto and cakes. It's also great for sauces, salsas, jams and honey: perfect for filling a hamper to take home.

### Formatgeria La Seu
C/Dagueria 16, Barri Gòtic; tel: 93 412 6548; www.formatgerialaseu.com; Tue–Sat 10am–2pm, 5–8pm; metro: Jaume I; map p.138 B3
Stocking only Spanish and Catalan cheeses and always sold at their prime, cheese lovers should not miss Katherine McLoughlin's wonderful walk-in dairy. You can try three cheeses with a glass of wine for under €5.

### Orolíquido
C/de la Palla 8, Barri Gòtic; tel: 93 302 2980; www.oroliquido.com; Tue–Sat 10am–2pm, 5–8pm; metro: Jaume I or Liceu; map p.138 B3
This designer store in olive green and slate stocks an impressive range of all-Spanish

olive oils and by-products. Friendly assistants are happy to let you try before you buy.

### Papabubble
C/Ample 28, Barri Gòtic; tel: 93 268 8625; www.papabubble.com; Tue–Fri 10am–2pm, 4–8.30pm, Sat 11am–7.30pm; metro: Barceloneta; map p.138 B2
A must for sweet-tooths, this seriously hip Aussie-owned handmade hard candy shop now has branches in New York, Tokyo and Amsterdam.

### Lavinia
Avda Diagonal 605, Eixample; tel: 93 363 4445; www.lavinia.es; Mon–Sat 10am–9pm; metro: maria Cristina; map p.132 C4
The most extensive wine selection in town in a cool modern setting is a must for serious wine buffs. They can also help you to ship it home.

### Vilaviniteca
C/Agullers 7, Born; tel: 93 268 3227; www.vilaviniteca.es; Mon–Sat 8.30am–8.30pm, Aug: till 2pm; metro: Jaume I; map p.138 B2
Smaller but no less impressive, this store is run by serious wine lovers who'll happily talk you through everything from a bottle of Torres to an obscure label from deepest, darkest Catalonia so long as they're talking wine. Tasting courses are also available if you're here for the long haul.

# Gay and Lesbian

Barcelona's aspirations to be the gay capital of Europe are still a long way from being achieved, but there are a variety of scenes that should appeal to all travellers. Conveniently centred around the Eixample (or Gaixample as it is also known), the most popular area is bordered by C/Diputació and Aragó to Balmes and Villarroel. Check out the free magazines available city-wide (*Shanguide* and *Nois* particularly) for a current picture of what's happening around the city. With a social scene worthy of its own book, the seaside town of Sitges is also worth checking out *(see also Around Barcelona, p.22–3)*.

## Where to Stay

### Hotel Axel
C/Arribau 33; tel: 93 323 9393; www.axelhotels.com; €€; metro: Universitat; map p.134 A2
The jewel in the crown as far as accommodation is concerned. This ultra-modern boutique hotel features minimalist décor and a rooftop sun terrace and jacuzzi that is as popular after dark as it is during the day.

## Where to Eat

### Castro
C/Casanova 85, Eixample; tel: 93 323 6784; www.castrorestaurant.com; Mon–Fri 1–4pm, 9pm–midnight, Sat 9pm–midnight; metro: Universitat; map p.133 E1
Almost an institution in Barcelona, Castro offers an eclectic menu set against stark, industrial surrounds. Sometimes leather-clad staff can appear intimidating, but they're softer than they seem and happy to guide you through a creative Mediterranean menu.

### Restaurant dDivine
C/Balmes 24; tel: 670 093 179; www.ddivine.com; Mon–Fri noon–4pm, Wed–Sat 10pm–2am; metro: Universitat; map p.134 A1
Barcelona Drag Queen (with a capital 'Q') Divine ensures a rip-roaring time and spectacular costume changes. Dinner is served efficiently between the bantering (in Spanish) and performances. Bookings for weekends recommended.

### Zoologic
C/Casanova 30; tel: 93 453 5259; www.zoologicrestaurant.com; Mon–Fri 1–4pm, 9pm–midnight, Sat 9pm–midnight; metro: Urgell; map p.137 E4
A spectacular fusion of space, food and entertainment, Zoologic offers an excellent, if somewhat pricey menu, served in intimate surroundings. Between courses, the food plays second fiddle to some stunning performances by a variety of drag queens and entertainers.

## Where to Drink

### Átame
C/Consell de Cent 257; tel: 93 454 9273; Mon–Thur, Sun 6.30pm–2.30am, Fri–Sat 6.30pm–3am; metro: Universitat; map p.133 E1
Divas dominate this bar, either appearing endlessly on the TV screens that pepper the walls, or live in the form of drag performances on Tuesdays, Thursdays and Sundays. Look out for the usual lip-synching turns, or the far more entertaining bitch fest slinging matches.

### La Concha
C/Guàrdia 14; tel: 93 302 4118; Mon–Thur, Sun 5pm–2.30am, Fri–Sat 5pm–3am; metro: Liceu; map p.138 A3
There aren't many bars that have that Marrakech kitsch feeling, but this place does it well. One part of the bar becomes a tiny dance floor at weekends, complete with impromptu belly dancing.

### People Lounge
C/Villarroel 71; tel: 93 532 7743; www.peoplebcn.com; daily 8pm–3am; metro: Urgell; map p.133 E1
Think chandeliers and candelabras, sophisticated cocktails and a backdrop of show tunes, and you have People

For more information, check online at www.barcelonagay.com and www.guiagay.com.

**Left:** gay-friendly restaurant Castro in the Eixample.

### Z:eltas

C/Casanova 75; tel: 93 451 8469; www.zeltas.net; daily 10pm–3am; metro: Universitat; map p.133 E1

Although open throughout the week, this stylish bar only really gets busy towards the weekend. A young, trendy crowd then packs the bar and crams itself onto the tiny dance floor to move and shake to the funky house beats.

### For the Girls

#### La Femme

C/Plató 13; Fri–Sat midnight–3am; metro: Lesseps or FGC Muntaner

An attractive, trendy crowd populates this busy 'boy-free' bar. Dance music, comfortable surroundings, and neon lighting completes the picture.

#### Kuit

C/Consell de Cent 280; www.kuitdisco.com; Thur–Sat midnight–5.30am; admission charge for men, women free; metro: Passeig de Gracia; map p.134 B2

From the owner of Z:eltas comes this new addition to the club scene. Happy house music means the dance floor is packed, while the stark black marble décor and mirrors satisfy even the most narcissistic of lipstick lesbians.

#### Prados (formerly Via)

C/María Cubi 4; Fri–Sat 11.30pm–5.30am; metro: Gràcia; map p.134 B4

A small, friendly haunt that has been a mainstay on the Barcelona lesbian scene for a number of years. The small dance floor fills quickly, especially as other bars close their doors for the night.

---

Away from the tank top clad Muscle Marys of the Gaixample, **La Penúltima** is a mixed (rather than exclusively gay) friendly bar situated in a converted bodega. *See also Bars and Cafés, p.31.*

---

Lounge. Worth visiting just to see the collection of Broadway and West End show posters that adorn the walls.

### Where to Party

#### Martins

Passeig de Gràcia 130; tel: 93 218 7167; www.martins-disco.com; Wed–Sun midnight–5am; admission charge; metro: Diagonal; map p.134 B2

The heir apparent to the late night scene, Martins offers three bars, a porno lounge, and decent-sized dance floor to attract a wide range of party *guapos* ready to play.

#### Metro

C/Sepúlveda 185; tel: 93 323 5227; www.metrodisco.bcn; Mon 1–5am, Tue–Sun midnight–5am; admission charge; metro: Universitat; map p.137 E4

With the closure of Salvation, the newly refurbished Metro has become a magnet for late-night frivolity. Two dark, pulsating dance floors provide either heavier house music or lighter Latin beats to keep punters entertained.

**Left:** club favourite, Metro.

# History

### c.15 BC

Roman soldiers found colony of Barcino on the Mons Taber hill, between the present-day Plaça Sant Jaume and cathedral.

### c. AD 350

Roman city walls built.

### 415

The Visigoths capture Barcelona. Their leader Ataulf temporarily makes it his capital.

### 711

The Moors invade Spain and capture Barcelona in 713.

### 801

The Franks, under Charlemagne's son Louis the Pious, take Barcelona and found the *Marca Hispànica* (Spanish March) in what would become Catalonia.

### c.880

Wilfred the Hairy (Guifré el Pelós), count of Ripoll, unifies the Catalan counties and establishes the House of Barcelona, a dynasty that lasts 500 years.

### 985

Al-Mansur, grand vizier of the caliph of Córdoba, sacks Barcelona.

### 988

Count Borrell II renounces all obligations to the kings of France after receiving no help against Al-Mansur, making Catalonia effectively independent.

### 1137

Count Berenguer IV of Barcelona marries Petronella, heiress to the throne of Aragón, forming the joint Catalan-Aragonese monarchy.

### c.1190

The *Usatges*, the Catalan legal code, is compiled and written in Catalan.

### 1213

Count-King Pere I is killed at the battle of Muret in Languedoc, and loses nearly all the monarchy's lands in southern France.

### 1229

Jaume I of Aragón takes Mallorca from Moorish rule, followed by Ibiza in 1235.

### 1238

Jaume I conquers Valencia.

### 1274

Barcelona's city government, the Consell de Cent, is established.

### 1298

Construction begins on the cathedral.

### 1300s

The Catalan-Aragonese monarchy extends its power over the Mediterranean to Sardinia and Sicily.

**1329**

Construction begins on Santa Maria del Mar.

**1336–87**

Under Pere III some of the greatest buildings of Catalan Gothic were built, including the Drassanes (Shipyards).

**1347–50**

Black Death kills half Barcelona's population.

**1359**

Corts Catalanes or Catalan Parliament established, with a council, the Generalitat de Catalunya, to administer finances.

**1391**

Anti-Jewish pogroms in Barcelona and throughout Aragón and Castile.

**1462–73**

Catalan civil war.

**1469**

Fernando II of Aragón marries Queen Isabel I of Castile, uniting all the Spanish Christian kingdoms in one inheritance.

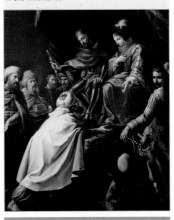

**1492**

Granada falls, Columbus discovers America, and all Jews are expelled from the Spanish kingdoms.

**1640**

Catalans rise in revolt against Felipe IV in the 'War of the Reapers' (Guerra dels Segadors), and the Generalitat places the country under the authority of French king Louis XIII.

61

**1652**
Spanish troops recapture Barcelona.

**1659**
In the Treaty of the Pyrenees, all of Catalonia north of the Pyrenees – Roussillon and Perpignan – is ceded to France.

**1702**
Barcelona sides with the Habsburg Archduke Charles in the War of Spanish Succession, against the French Bourbon Felipe V.

**1714**
French and Spanish troops take the city after a year-long siege on 11 September.

**1715–16**
The victorious Felipe V abolishes the remaining Catalan institutions and establishes Spain as a single, centralised state. In Barcelona half La Ribera district is destroyed to make space for a fortress, the Ciutadella.

**1808–14**
Napoleon's troops occupy most of Spain, including Barcelona.

**1814**
Fernando VII is restored to power. Barcelona's trade and industry start a steady expansion.

**1836–8**
Dissolution of most of Barcelona's monasteries, opening up large areas for new building.

**1842**
Barcelona is bombarded from Montjuïc to suppress a radical revolt.

**1854–6**
The Ciutadella and the medieval city walls are demolished.

**1860**
Work begins on the city's new grid (Eixample), designed by Ildefons Cerdà.

**1868–73**
September Revolution, against Queen Isabel II, begins six years of agitation. The first anarchist groups are formed.

**1873**
Spain briefly becomes a republic.

**1882**
Building of Sagrada Família begins.

**1888**
Barcelona hosts its first Universal Exhibition.

**1909**
During the Setmana Tràgica (Tragic Week) churches are destroyed in riots after the government tries to conscript extra troops for its colonial war in Morocco.

**1923–30**
Military dictatorship of Primo de Rivera suppresses unions and Catalan freedoms.

**1929**
A second Universal Exhibition is held on Montjuïc. The Plaça d'Espanya, Palau Nacional and Poble Espanyol are all built.

**1931**
Second Spanish Republic proclaimed: Catalonia is given autonomy, with a restored Generalitat under Francesc Macià.

**1936–9**
Spanish Civil War: after three years of bitter fighting and destruction, Barcelona falls to Franco's right-wing armies on 26 January 1939.

**1959–60**
After years of scarcity, local economy begins to revive as tourism and foreign investment enter Spain.

**1975**
Franco dies on 20 November.

**1977–8**
First democratic general elections since 1936, and first local elections, won in Barcelona by socialists. Catalan autonomy statute granted and Catalan recognised as official language.

**1980**
Jordi Pujol is elected first president of restored Catalan Generalitat.

**1982**
Pasqual Maragall becomes mayor of Barcelona.

**1992**
City is transformed for the Olympic Games, which are a huge success.

**1997**
Maragall resigns and is succeeded by Joan Clos.

**2003**
Jordi Pujol retires; Pasqual Maragall becomes Generalitat President at head of a left-wing coalition.

**2004**
Socialists led by José Luis Rodríguez Zapatero take over Spanish central government after Partido Popular is discredited by its response to 11 March Al-Qaeda bombings in Madrid.

**2006**
Maragall coalition collapses, but after elections a similar coalition takes over the Generalitat, led by fellow socialist José Montilla. Jordi Hereu becomes mayor when Clos is made Spanish Minister for Industry, Commerce and Tourism.

63

# Hotels

For the first half of the noughties it seemed that every new hotel in Barcelona was a four-star or above, turning it from a cheap, bohemian getaway to a prohibitively expensive weekend jaunt. Happily savvy hoteliers have realised that not all visitors have money to burn and have set about providing something more accessible. In 2006 and 2007 the majority of new openings were of the cheap and chic variety: trendy digs with a good scattering of rooms for under 100 euros a night. Prices still reflect the fact that Barcelona is seen as a weekend destination, but now it has something for most budgets.

### Plaça de Catalunya and La Rambla

**Hotel 1898**
La Rambla 109; tel: 93 552 9552; www.nnhotels.es; €€€€; metro: Catalunya or Liceu; map p.138 B4

This five-star boutique hotel occupies the old Philippine Tobacco Factory that was located here at the turn of the century. Huge black-and-white photos tell the story on each floor against a backdrop of candy-striped wallpaper, while the exclusive basement revives weary travellers with 'gold therapy' and 'walking on clouds' massages. If you have €1,500 to splash, suite 501 is one of the best in the city, with a private pool, but the hotel also has a communal roof garden and swimming pool for those of lesser means.

**Rivoli Ramblas**
La Rambla 128; tel: 93 481 7676; www.rivolihotels.com; €€€; metro: Catalunya or Liceu; map p.138 B4

Behind the elegantly cool 1930s façade is a modern hotel with tasteful rooms. The barman of the Blue Moon cocktail bar downstairs plays great music, and it's not a bad place to kick off the night.

### Barri Gòtic

**Bonic B&B**
C/Josep Anslem Clavé 9, 1º4ª; tel: 626 053 434; www.bonic-barcelona.com; €; metro: Drassanes; map p.138 A2

This friendly eight-room guesthouse mixes Moroccan and Mediterranean styles to create a secret hideaway wedged between the port and the Old Quarter. It has a pleasant lounge and dining area, but the three scrupulously clean bathrooms are communal.

**Duquesa de Cardona**
Passeig Colom 12; tel: 93 268 9090; www.hduquesadecardona.com; €€€; metro: Drassanes; map p.138 B2

A wonderfully romantic hotel housed in one of the old mansion blocks giving on to the original waterfront and the old harbour. Bedrooms are small but sweet, and the pool and roof terrace, available for

**Left:** the futuristic lobby at Hotel Silken Diagonal.

orientals.com; €€; metro: Jaume I; map p.138 B3

For many years this was the coolest affordable boutique in town, but the competition is now stiff enough to have toppled the Banys from its lead. It still has plenty of class though, from its downtown location to its elegant rooms, fresh flowers and spacious, loft-style rooms a couple of doors along.

### Chic & Basic

C/Princesa 50 entresuelo; tel: 93 295 4650; www.chicandbasic.com; metro: Jaume I; map p.139 C3

The white-on-white interior of this budget boutique gives it the air of a 1970s photo shoot. It is retro without really meaning to be, fun-loving and unstuffy with a liberal sprinkling of porn-star glamour to serve as your weekend base.

private parties, are pure gold in this part of town.

### H10 Racó del Pi

C/Pi 7; tel: 93 342 6190; www.h10hotels.es; €€€; metro: Liceu; map p.138 B3

Set just off the delightful Plaça del Pi, this small hotel occupies an old palace and radiates loveliness. A glass of cava on arrival, for example is a nice touch, and unlike in much of the Gothic Quarter, rooms are spacious and airy.

### Hotel Catedral

C/dels Capellans 4; tel: 93 304 2255; www.barcelonacatedral.com; €€–€€€; metro: Jaume I; map p.138 B3

Modern, sleek and conservatively sexy, this new Barri Gòtic pad has bags of understated class. Designer sofas against a bamboo garden bring unpretentious elegance. A programme of cooking classes and wine tastings keep galloping gourmets amused, while a good-sized rooftop pool and gym provide somewhere to work it off.

**Left:** the rooftop pool at Hotel 1898.

### Hotel Neri

C/Sant Sever 5; tel: 93 304 0655; www.hotelneri.com; €€€€; metro: Jaume I; map p.138 B3

With its castle-like Gothic walls, stone staircase and plush red velvet sofas, the Neri is probably the most romantic hotel in town. You'll find candles, incense and chocolates in the bedrooms, a secret garden on the roof and a gourmet restaurant spilling onto one of the city's loveliest plazas. No wonder John Malkovich likes it.

### Levante

Baixada de Sant Miquel 2; tel: 93 317 9565; www.hostallevante.com; €; metro: Liceu or Jaume I; map p.138 B3

A friendly backpackers' haunt with a lively history. So the story goes, the young Picasso was a frequent visitor in the hostal's former life as a brothel, which inspired his painting *Les Demoiselles d'Avignon*.

## Sant Pere and Born

### Banys Orientals

C/Argenteria 37; tel: 93 268 8460; www.hotelbanys

**Making the most of your euro:**
These days, if you are looking for a cheap mini-break in Barcelona you are likely to be disappointed. Only the most basic of accommodations cost less than €50 a night, and prices can fluctuate. During a big trade fair like 3GSM or Bread and Butter you can expect prices to rise considerably. Ditto in high season: May and June, September and October, and December. Time your visit for quieter months, or mid-week, and you may get substantial discounts, as is likely if you choose a more business-orientated hotel for the weekend. A recent trend is to grade prices according to occupancy, so what costs you €100 one week, may well go up or down the next. And it is always worth checking the website for deals.

**Left:** Hotel Ciutat Vella's jacuzzi; **Below:** Casa Camper.

## Hotel Park
Avda Marquès de l'Argentera 11; tel: 93 319 6000; www.park hotelbarcelona.com; €€; metro: Barceloneta; map p.138 C2
Something of a landmark hotel for lovers of modernist architecture; more discerning guests may find the Park a little jaded. The chrome and mosaic-tiled bar, however, is fab for a pre-dinner cocktail, and the spiral staircase is movie star-worthy if you have something suitable to sashay in.

## Pensió 2000
C/Sant Pere Més Alt 6-1º; tel: 93 310 7466; www.pensio2000.com; €€; metro: Urquinaona; map p.138 B4
A noble marble staircase leads to this friendly home-from-home guesthouse. Clean, cheerful and spacious rooms make it excellent value for money, though in most cases you will need to share a bathroom. It is worth booking a room with a view of the Palau de la Música Catalana (see p.80).

## Raval

## Casa Camper
C/Elizabets 11; tel: 93 342 6280; www.casacamper.com; €€€; metro: Catalunya; map p.138 A4
Walk this way folks – the Mallorcan shoe manufacturer's hotel is as is as off-the-wall as its shoes. Think industrial minimalism mixed up with a spot of Shaker-inspired furniture and a splash of beach-hut chic. You will find the TV across the hall in your own private living room complete with hammock, and 'room service' in a free, help-yourself pod downstairs.

## Gat Xino
C/Hospital 155; tel: 93 324 8833; www.gataccommodation.

## Grand Hotel Central
Via Laietana 30; tel: 93 295 7900; www.grandhotelcentral.com; €€€; metro Jaume I; map p.138 B3
The jewel in the crown of this hotel is the rooftop infinity pool, and if rubbing shoulders with the fashion pack is your thing, this is the place for you. The grey-black décor of the rooms gives it a vamp-ish feel, and high-tech plasma TVs and DVD players are an added luxury for watching movies in bed.

## Hostal Girona
C/Girona 21, 1º1ª; tel: 93 265 0259; www.hostalgirona.com; €; metro: Urquinaona; map p.138 C4

Prices for an average double room:
€ under €100
€€ €100–€200
€€€ €200–€350
€€€€ over €350

The most famous little hostal in town, thanks to its *Almodóvar*-style décor: all gilded mirrors and Persian rugs against a backdrop of tiles and intricate cornicing. Rooms come in all guises, so take time to peruse the website, depending on whether you want a light-filled enclosed balcony, private bathroom or just something cheap.

## Hotel Ciutat
Carrer de la Princesa 35; tel: 93 269 7475; www.ciutathotels.com; €€; metro: Jaume I; map p.138 C3
Boutique on a budget in the heart of Barcelona's trendy Born neighbourhood. Rooms are small but sleek, with designer touches and decent toiletries. There is a plunge pool on the roof along with a small bar, and a restaurant downstairs.

com; €; metro: Universitat; map p.137 E3

The smarter of the two Gats, all 34 rooms here are individually decorated in bright, bright, skater-chic tones. A smart interior patio is great for sunny, relaxed breakfasts and also mark it out from the sister site. One of the best deals in town.

(Gat Raval is at C/Joaquim Costa 44, 10; tel: 93 441 6670; map p.134 B4).

### Hosteria Grau

C/Ramelleres 27; tel: 93 301 8135; www.hostalgrau.com; €; metro: Catalunya; map p.138 A4

This cute and cosy pension has a laid-back rhythm and a whole lot of soul. A recent facelift means communal areas and bedrooms are looking more spruce than ever, with exposed beams, lanterns and buttermilk walls. Hearty breakfasts are served in the adjoining bar.

### Hotel Ciutat Vella

C/Tallers 66; tel: 93 481 3799; www.hotelciutatvella.com; €; metro: Universitat or Catalunya; map p.138 A4

Situated on one of the Raval's hippest streets, this place is perfect for cash-

strapped disco queens: rates are determined by demand. All 40 rooms (some sleep up to six) are cheery, with crisp cotton sheets and cherry-red accents, but the *pièce de résistance* is the rooftop jacuzzi bubbling away at 30°C year-round.

### Hotel España

C/Sant Pau 9; tel: 93 318 1758; www.hotelespanya.com; €€; metro: Liceu; map p.138 A3

Magnificent Modernista décor on the ground floor by Domènech i Montaner is set off by kitsch touches and the 1950s-style bar. It is worth specifying that you want a room with original tiles or one that opens onto the interior patio. And understand that if you just call in for lunch, you're here for the décor, not the food.

### Hotel Peninsular

C/Sant Pau; tel: 93 302 3138; www.hpeninsular.com; €; metro: Liceu; map p.138 A3

A basic but pleasant enough *hostal* located in a former convent. The tiled floors and

impressive atrium ringed by balconies dripping with ferns make it a magical place to write your postcards, study the guidebook and make new friends. Watch your valuables, as thefts have been reported.

### Mesón de Castilla

C/ Valldonzella 5; tel: 93 318 2182; www.mesoncastilla.com; €€€; Universitat or Catalunya; map p.138 A4

Quite unlike anything else in town, this is a good bet for seasoned travellers sick to the back teeth of designer boutiques. Furniture is dark and old-fashioned, lace doilies decorate table-tops, intricate rugs soften vast reception rooms. Yet the bedrooms, for all their quirkiness, give a sense of being at home, and the lushly planted interior terrace where breakfast is served is a delight.

### The Waterfront and Poblenou

### Hostal Poblenou

Carrer Taulat 30 pral; tel: 93 221 2601; www.hostalpoblenou.com;

**Right:** Hotel España's Modernista restaurant.

€; metro: Poblenou

The *barrio's* moment has yet to come, though hip bars, restaurants and clubs are gradually finding their way here. Check in to this charming B&B if you are after serious beach hours (the city's finest are minutes away). It has five bright, airy rooms, Internet access, terrace, unlimited tea and coffee and darling hosts. Oh, and it is miles from the nearest stag or hen group.

**Hotel AB Skipper**

Avda del Litoral 10; tel: 93 221 6565; www.hotelabskipper.com; €€€; metro: Ciutadella-Vila Olímpica; map p.139 D2

This new American-style

---

Prices for an average double room:

€ under €100
€€ €100–€200
€€€ €200–€350
€€€€ over €350

---

five-star has all the boxes ticked. Facilities include several restaurants and bars, generous-sized rooms, two swimming pools, wellness spa and gym, various tours and sea views. It is great if you want your hand held as much as possible, or just want to chill out and not go anywhere at all.

**Hotel Arts**

C/Marina 19–21; tel: 93 221 1000; www.ritzcarlton.com; €€€€; metro: Ciutadella-Vila Olímpica; map p.139 D1

There is nowhere quite like the Arts in Barcelona. Not just because it is the tallest building in town; or because it has a **Six Senses Spa** in the penthouse; or even because it is where all the celebs stay. But because it's got that five-star feeling just right. With a mix of trendy and gourmet restaurants, a pool with a sea view and hammocks on the lawn, this is the place to stay when

you feel you have made it.
SEE ALSO PAMPERING, P.99; TAPAS BARS, P.121

**Hotel 54**

Passeig Joan de Borbó 54; tel: 93 325 0054; www.hotel54 barcelona.com; €€; metro: Barceloneta; map p.138 B1

There is a surprising dearth of accommodation in Barceloneta, so the opening of this chic little pleasure palace in 2007 was a no-brainer. Dove-grey rooms with neon splashes give it an Ibiza-style ambience, while the planted roof terrace with views of the boats has become the cocktail bar of choice for summer revellers.

**Rafael Diagonal Port**

C/Lope de Vega 4; tel: 93 230 2000; www.rafaelhoteles.com; €€€; tram: 4 Forum

This ultra-modern hotel is located on the beach at the hip new urban resort of Diag-

---

**Right:** Granados 83.

**Left:** Hotel Arts and Frank Gehry's copper fish sculpture.

onal Mar, making it a good choice for those doing the festival circuit in style: Summercase, Wintercase and Sónar *(see p.50 and 51)* are all hosted nearby at the Forum grounds. It is worth the extra to get a sea view.

**Sea Point Hostel**
Plaça del Mar 4; tel: 93 224 7075; www.seapointhostel.com; €; metro: Barceloneta; map p.138 C2
An unbeatable position for a youth hostel right on Barceloneta beach. This forward-thinking chain of cheap and cheerful youth hostels also has a branch in La Ribera – Gothic Point – and one on Passeig de Gràcia, Centric Point.

**Montjuïc, Poble Sec and Sant Antoni**

**AC Miramar**
Plaza Carlos Ibáñez 3, Passeig de Miramar, Montjuïc; tel: 93 281 1600; www.ac-hotels.com; €€€€; metro: Paral·lel then Funicular Montjuïc; map p.137 D2
Boasting an enviable position at the top of Montjuïc mountain, this upscale hotel is surrounded by green lawns and orange patios. The pool is lit by fibre optics to give the sensation of swimming in the

**Going it alone:** Increasingly visitors are opting to rent their own space in the city, which gives greater freedom in terms of eating and drinking and often works out cheaper. Among the best are www.destinationbcn.com, who offer beautiful, individually designed apartments. www.apartmentsinbarcelona.com specialise in digs with a terrace, and www.bcn-rentals.com cover accommodation for larger groups.

stars, and curiously the best room is actually the cheapest: a small double at the top with a hot tub on the terrace.

**B-Hotel**
Gran Via 389–391; tel: 93 552 9500; www.nnhotels.com; €€€; metro: Espanya; map p.133 C1
With its slick design and utterly fabulous rooftop infinity pool, one can't help wishing that the B-Hotel was positioned somewhere just a little bit quieter. Traffic noise from the intersection of Plaça Espanya and the Gran Via is full on. If you don't mind a smaller room at the back of the hotel you should get a decent night's sleep, and it is a top location if you are in town for one of the trade fairs. In the lobby there is a good wine and tapas bar.

**Market Hotel**
C/Comte Borrell 68; tel: 93 325 1205; www.markethotel.com.es; €€; metro: Sant Antoni or Urgell; map p.137 D4
The meteoric rise of this smart Asian-themed boutique off the beaten path is testament to its popularity. It can be murder to get in here. But when you consider a spacious suite with a double-bed-sized tub and walled-in terrace can be yours for under €120, romantic mini-breaks are suddenly twice as attractive. It has a restaurant; no room service.

**The Eixample**

**Granados 83**
C/Enric Granados 83; tel: 93 492 9670; www.derbyhotels.com; €€; metro: Diagonal; map p.134 A3
A taste of New York in the upper Eixample, this smart townhouse is situated on a leafy, partially pedestrianised street full of hip bars and restaurants. Red brick and steel offset plush furnishings and a super-sexy environment peopled by occasional celebrities and the young jet set. Extras include a designer vodka bar, rooftop pool bar, terrace restaurant and WiFi.

**Habitat Sky**
C/ Pere IV 272; tel: 93 492 9394; www.habitathotelsky.com; €€€€; metro: Poblenou

**Left:** Casa Fuster.

club and somewhere in between, **Spaciomm**, a spa.
SEE ALSO PAMPERING, P.99

### Hotel Pulitzer
C/Bergara 8; tel: 93 481 6767; www.hotelpulitzer.es; €€€; metro: Catalunya or Universitat; map p.138 B4

A vast lounge bar, generously furnished with deep sofas and armchairs, has made this something of a cocktail destination even for those not staying at the hotel. It has a certain big-city feel about it, though the plush rooms are on the small size. A rooftop that fizzes with summer parties more than makes up for it by making outsiders feel like locals.

### Hotel Regina
C/Bergara 4; tel: 93 301 3232; www.hotelregina.com; €€; metro: Catalunya; map p.134 B1

From the old school of cool, the Regina is sumptuous without being stuffy, arty without being pompous, central yet removed from the main tourist drag. Rooms are spacious and stylish, and the elegant cocktail bar and lounge in the lobby give added luxe factor. Guests also get free entry to the nearby Holmes Place gym.

### Hotel Silken Diagonal Barcelona
Avda Diagonal 205; tel: 93 489 5300; www.hoteldiagonal barcelona.com; €€€; metro: Glories

Located in a fairly non-descript part of town, the high design of this hotel points to an altogether brighter future. Designed by local boy Juli Capella, think Stanley Kubrick-style interiors with the boldest views possible of Jean Nouvel's

Standing at 120 metres (394ft) high, this is the hot new designer opening of 2008. Spectacular use of light and space, three gourmet restaurants, luxury spa, swimming pool and garden, a night in 'space' does not come cheap, but it is a must for design and architecture aficionados.

### Hotel Constanza
C/Bruc 33; tel: 93 270 1910; www.hotelconstanza.com; €€; metro: Urquinaona; map p.134 C1

A chic hotel influenced by the Japanese aesthetic: think paper screens decorated with orchids, pebble paintings and

water features. It is also one of the few places in town that goes out of its way to welcome lone travellers, offering special rates and single rooms that are actually pleasant places to be. Some of the larger rooms have private terraces, which are worth asking for when booking.

### Hotel Omm
C/Rosselló 265; tel: 93 445 4000; www.hotelomm.es; €€€€; metro: Passeig de Gràcia; map p.134 B3

Pleasure seekers need look no further than the Omm, the city's hottest, most hedonistic hotel. An open-plan lobby reveals a lounge, healthy snack bar and Moo, a two Michelin-starred restaurant. Futuristic hallways reveal sleek and lovely rooms with two bathrooms. The rooftop boasts a pool with views over Gaudí's La Pedrera just next door, the basement a night-

> Prices for an average double room:
> € under €100
> €€ €100–€200
> €€€ €200–€350
> €€€€ over €350

**Right and above:** designer heaven at Hotel Omm.

> **Costa Brava dreaming:** This stretch of wild and lovely coastline is peppered with tiny coves and great walks. From the same people who brought you the Market Hotel in the Raval, are two boutiques that won't break the bank: **La Malcontenta** (Paratge Torre Mirona, Platja de Castell 12, Palamós; tel: 97 231 2330; www.lamalcontenta.com; €€), a country estate situated among rolling hills; and **Hotel Trias** (Passeig del Mar s/n, Palamós; tel: 97 260 1800, www.hoteltrias.com; €€), a modern block on the beach.

luminescent Torre Agbar *(see p.27)* from the rooftop pool.

### Soho Hotel
Gran Via de les Corts Catalanes 543–545; tel: 93 552 9610; www.nnhotels.com, €€€; metro: Urgell; map p.133 E1
Designed by the Catalan Alfredo Arribas with a comfortable yet minimalist theme, this is a good choice for design junkies on a budget. Verner Panton lamps and funky Moare glasswork streamlined through the interior give it an edge over Ikea boutiques. A wood-decked roof terrace and pool add extra spark. No restaurant.

### Upper Neighbourhoods

**Anita's B&B**
C/August Font 24; tel: 93 254 6793; www.anitasbarcelona.com; €; metro: Tibidabo
A stylish B&B situated high up in the city with fabulous views. All three rooms are light and airy, with spectacular balconies. Super-friendly service includes use of a dining room, lounge and terrace. An optional airport pick-up/ drop-off service is also available.

### Casa Fuster
Passeig de Gràcia 132; tel: 93 255 3000; www.hotelcasa fuster.com; €€€€; metro: Diagonal; map p.134 B3
For those extravagant of wallet, Casa Fuster is where it's at. A somewhat controversial project, this ornately decorated Modernista hotel once belonged to an aristocratic family, and many felt that the property should have remained in the public domain. You can duck in for a peek at the **Café Viennese** if you can't afford to stay here. If you can, rooms are on the small side, but you are getting your own slice of history.
SEE ALSO BARS AND CAFÉS, P.35

### Gran Hotel La Florida
Ctra Vallvidrera a Tibidabo 83–89; tel: 93 259 3000; www.hotellaflorida.com; €€€€; Perched high on Tibidabo hill, this grand de luxe hotel was brought back to life from its former glory in the 1940s

when the likes of Ernest Hemingway and James Stewart used to stay here. It is a schlep from town, but this can sometimes work to your advantage: stunning terraced gardens, a spectacular indoor-outdoor infinity pool trickling over the mountainside, gourmet restaurant and spa are sometimes wrapped up in *loco* deals.

# Language

**B**arcelona has long been a bilingual city, despite the efforts of various oppressors to smother Catalan. Franco's was the most recent attempt, but since his death in 1975 the language has gone from strength to strength, overtaking Spanish as the lingua franca of business and education, as well as the language that most *barcelonins* use at home. It should not be confused with a dialect, and has as much in common with Italian, French or Portuguese as it does with Castilian Spanish. The following chapter provides some key words and phrases in both languages.

## Catalan

Catalan can be harder to follow than Spanish, as words and sounds tend to run into one another as they do in English. One oddity is the l·l, pronounced as a slightly more emphatic l, while ll is pronounced – as in Spanish – as the *lli* in million. The unstressed **e** sounds much as it does in English (like the e in written), while an unstressed **o** is pronounced **oo**. Note that **t** is silent at the end of a word, after **l** or **n**, or before a consonant.

## Useful Words/Phrases

**GENERAL**
yes *sí*
no *no*
please *si us plau*
thank you (very much) *(moltes) gràcies*
you're welcome *de res*
excuse me *perdoni*
hello *hola*
good morning *bon dia*
good afternoon *bona tarda*
good evening/night *bona nit*
goodbye *adéu*
How much is it? *Quant val?*
What is your name? *Com es diu?*

OK *d'acord*
My name is… *Em dic…*
Do you speak English? *Parla anglès?*
I am English/American *Sóc anglès (anglesa)/americà/ana*
I don't understand *No ho entenc*
Please speak more slowly *Parli més a poc a poc, sisplau*
Can you help me? *Em pot ajudar?*
I'm looking for… *Estic buscant…*
Where is…? *On és…?*
I'm sorry *Ho sento*
I don't know *No ho sé*
See you tomorrow *Fins demà*
See you soon *Fins aviat*
When? *Quan?*
What time is it? *Quina hora és?*
here *aquí*

there *allà*
left *esquerra*
right *dreta*
straight on *tot recte*
far *lluny*
near *a prop*
opposite *al davant*
beside *al costat*
today *avui*
yesterday *ahir*
tomorrow *demà*
now *ara*
later *més tard/després*
this morning *aquest matí*
this afternoon *aquesta tarda*
tonight *aquesta nit*

**ON ARRIVAL**
I want to get off at… *Voldria baixar a…*
Is there a bus to…? *Hi ha un autobús cap a…?*
Which line do I take for…? *Quina línia agafo per…?*
airport *l'aeroport*
railway station *l'estació de tren*
bus station *l'estació d'autobusos*
metro stop *la parada de metro*
bus *l'autobús*
bus stop *la parada d'autobús*
platform *l'andana*
ticket *un bitllet*

**Left:** street signs are shown in Catalan and Castellano.

size (shoes) *el número*
receipt *el tiquet*
chemist *la farmàcia*
bakery *el forn de pa*
book shop *la llibreria*
department store *els grans magatzems*
grocery *el botiga de queviures*
tobacconist *l'estanc*
market *el mercat*
supermarket *el supermercat*

### SIGHTSEEING

tourist information office *oficina de turisme*
free *gratuït*
open *obert*
closed *tancat*
every day *tots els dias*
all year *tot l'any*
all day *tot el dia*
to book *reservar*
town map *el plànol*
road map *el mapa de carreteres*

### DINING OUT

breakfast *l'esmorzar*
lunch *el dinar*
dinner *el sopar*
meal *el menjar*
first course *el primer plat*
main course *el segon plat*
dessert *les postres*
set menu *el menú del dia*
drink included *beguda inclosa*
wine list *la carta de vins*
red wine *vi negre*

return ticket *un bitllet de anada i tornada*
toilets *els lavabos/serveis*
I'd like a (single/double) room *Voldria una habitació (individual/doble)*
with shower *amb dutxa*
with bath *amb banyera*
Is breakfast included? *L'esmorzar està inclòs?*
bed *el llit*
key *la clau*
lift *l'ascensor*
air-conditioning *l'aire condicionat*

### EMERGENCIES

Help! *Auxili!*
Stop! *Pari!*

Where is the nearest telephone? *On és el telèfon més proper?*
Where is the nearest hospital? *On és l'hospital més proper?*
I am sick *Em trobo malament*
I have lost my passport/ wallet *He perdut el passaport/la cartera*

### SHOPPING

I'd like to buy… *Voldria comprar…*
How much is it? *Quant val?*
Do you take credit cards? *Es pot pagar amb targeta?*
I'm just looking *Estic mirant*
size (clothes) *la talla*

white wine *vi blanc*
the bill *el compte*
fork *la forquilla*
knife *el ganivet*
spoon *la cullera*
teaspoon *la culereta*
plate *el plat*
glass *la copa* (for wine),
*el vas* (for water)
I am a vegetarian
*Sóc vegetarià/ana*
I'd like to order *Voldria
demanar*
tax included *IVA inclòs*
Enjoy your meal! *Bon profit!*

## AT THE MARKET

beef *vedella*
lamb *xai*
chicken *pollastre*
fish *peix*
shellfish *marisc*
potato *patata*
tomato *tomàquet*
carrot *pastanaga*
garlic *all*
onion *ceba*
mushroom *xampinyó*
apple *poma*
orange *taronja*
pear *pera*
banana *plàtan*

## Castellano

Spanish is the easiest to pro-
nounce of all Romance languages, with each letter
having a consistent and inde-
pendently pronounced sound.
Some letters to watch out for
are **j**, or **g** when followed by **i**
or **e** (pronounced like the *ch*

in the Scottish loch); **z**, or **c**
when followed by **i** or **e** (a soft
**th**); **ll** (like *lli* in million), and **ñ**
(like *ni* in onion).

## Useful Words/Phrases

### GENERAL

yes *sí*
no *no*
please *por favor*
thank you (very much)
*(muchas) gracias*
you're welcome *de nada*
excuse me *perdón*
hello *hola*
good morning *buenos días*
good afternoon *buenas tardes*
good evening/night *buenas
noches*
goodbye *adiós*
OK *vale*
How much is it? *¿Cuánto
vale?*
What is your name? *¿Cómo
se llama?*
My name is… *Me llamo…*
Do you speak English?
*¿Habla inglés?*
I am English/American
*Soy inglés (inglesa)/
Americano/a*
I don't understand
*No lo entiendo*
Please speak more slowly
*Hable más despacio,
por favor*
Can you help me? *¿Puede
ayudarme?*
I'm looking for… *Estoy
buscando…*
Where is…? *¿Dónde está?*
I'm sorry *Lo siento*

I don't know *No lo sé*
See you tomorrow *Hasta
mañana*
See you soon *Hasta pronto*
When? *¿Cuándo?*
What time is it?
*¿Qué hora es?*
here *aquí*
there *allí*
left *izquierda*
right *derecha*
straight on *todo recto*
far *lejos*
near *cerca*
opposite *en frente*
beside *al lado*
today *hoy*
yesterday *ayer*
tomorrow *mañana*
now *ahora*
later *más tarde*
this morning *esta mañana*
this afternoon *esta tarde*
tonight *esta noche*

### ON ARRIVAL

I want to get off at…
*Quiero bajar en…*
Is there a bus to…?
*Hay un autobús que
vaya a…?*
Which line do I take for…?
*Qué línea tengo que
coger para…?*
airport *el aeropuerto*
railway station *la estación
de ferrocarril*
bus station *la estación de
autobuses*
metro stop *la parada de
metro*
bus *el autobús*

bus stop *la parada de autobús*
platform *el andén*
ticket *el billete*
return ticket *el billete de ida y vuelta*
toilets *los servicios/lavabos*
I'd like a (single/double) room *Quería una habitación (individual/doble)*
…with shower *con ducha*
…with bath *con bañera*
Is breakfast included? *¿Está incluído el desayuno?*
bed *la cama*
key *la llave*
lift *el ascensor*
air-conditioning *aire acondicionado*

## EMERGENCIES

Help! *¡Socorro!*
Stop! *¡Pare!*
Where is the nearest telephone? *¿Dónde está el teléfono más cercano?*
Where is the nearest hospital? *¿Dónde está el hospital más cercano?*
I am sick *Estoy enfermo/a*
I have lost my passport/wallet *He perdido mi pasaporte/cartera*

## SHOPPING

I'd like to buy… *Quiero comprar…*
How much is it? *¿Cuánto vale?*
Do you take credit cards? *¿Se aceptan tarjetas de crédito?*

### Days of the Week (Castellano)
Monday *Lunes*
Tuesday *Martes*
Wednesday *Miércoles*
Thursday *Jueves*
Friday *Viernes*
Saturday *Sábado*
Sunday *Domingo*

I'm just looking *Estoy mirando*
size (clothes) *la talla*
size (shoes) *el número*
receipt *el tiquet*
chemist *la farmacia*
bakery *la panadería*
book shop *la librería*
department store *los grandes almacenes*
grocery *el colmado*
tobacconist *el estanco*
market *el mercado*
supermarket *el supermercado*

## SIGHTSEEING

tourist information office *la oficina de turismo*
free *gratis/gratuito*
open *abierto*
closed *cerrado*
every day *todos los días*
all year *todo el año*
all day *todo el día*
to book *reservar*
town map *el plano*
road map *el mapa de carreteras*

## DINING OUT

breakfast *el desayuno*
lunch *la comida/la almuerzo*
dinner *la cena*

meal *la comida*
first course *el entrante*
main course *el segundo*
dessert *el postre*
set menu *el menú del día*
drink included *bebida incluída*
wine list *la carta de vinos*
red wine *vino tinto*
white wine *vino blanco*
the bill *la cuenta*
fork *el tenedor*
knife *el cuchillo*
spoon *la cuchara*
teaspoon *la cucharilla*
plate *el plato*
glass *la copa* (for wine), *el vaso* (for water)
I am a vegetarian *Soy vegetariano/a*
I'd like to order *Me gustaría pedir*
tax included *IVA incluído*
Enjoy your meal! *Que aproveche!*

## AT THE MARKET

beef *ternera*
lamb *cordero*
chicken *pollo*
fish *pescado*
shellfish *marisco*
potato *patata*
tomato *tomate*
carrot *zanahoria*
garlic *ajo*
onion *cebolla*
mushroom *champiñón*
apple *manzana*
orange *naranja*
pear *pera*
banana *plátano*

# Literature

It is a shame that the books most people have heard of that document the history and culture of Barcelona and her people, are often written by foreigners. The city has a rich tradition of great writers, poets and playwrights, and at the turn of the 20th century it was as much an intellectual hothouse as Paris. At its peak in the 1950s the majority of Catalan writers, like Eduardo Mendoza, Manuel Vásquez Montalbán and Luis Goytisolo, were vehemently anti-Franco and fought hard to forge their own autonomy in terms of literature, yet even they were forced to write in Spanish under the Franco regime.

## Medieval Writing

There were several influential Catalan writers at this time, among them Barcelona native Bernat Metge, Ramon Llull, Ausiàs March – you will see that their names have been taken by streets all over the region – and Joanot Martorell, who wrote the great romance *Tirant lo Blanc*, which also happened to be the last major work to be written in the Catalan language until the 19th century.

Yet the most famous book to come out of this period was the *Llibre de Sent Soví*, published in 1324, which was Europe's first recipe book and is available as the *Book of Sent Soví* to this day. It was written anonymously and contains 222 recipes.

## Civil War Writing

The decades following the Civil War were the brightest in terms of people expressing what they knew and felt. It not only brought out the prevailing mood of the Catalans, but attracted foreign writers like George Orwell, Gerald Brenan, Ernest Hemingway and

Barcelona has a handful of significant literary festivals: **Poesía** is a seven-day international festival of poetry (from the start of May). **Diada de Sant Jordi** on 23 April *(see also Festivals, p.49)* pays homage to the city's literary vitality. **Kosmopolis** is a biennial festival in October that looks at contemporary world literature and how we consume it.

Martha Gellhorn in their droves to document what was happening in Spain. Those painful years have continued to inspire people ever since.

Books published at this time include Mercè Rodoreda's extraordinary tale *The Time of the Doves* (1962), telling the story of a young woman who falls in love during the Civil War and what happens thereafter, and Carmen Laforet's autobiographical novel, named *Andrea* in English, which describes the prevailing mood during the war. But the most widely read Catalan writer of all time is the late Josep Pla, whose social and cultural commentaries before and after the Civil War, and towards the end of his life, *Gastronomy*, have formed the basis for so much that is written today.

## Contemporary Writing

Quim Monzó is currently Catalonia's best-selling author, despite his rather tawdry scenes and black sense of humour. *The Enormity of Tragedy*, about a boy growing up in post-Civil War Barcelona, was translated into English in 2007.

Juan Goytisolo, born in the city in 1931 and widely agreed to be Spain's greatest living writer, recently penned *The Garden of Secrets* (1997; available in English), which tells the story of the homosexual Eusebio from 28 different perspectives.

Recent festivals are starting to encourage younger writers, notably Jordi Puntí for his writing on love and sex, to find their niche.

## Great Reads

**Barcelona** by Robert Hughes; the definitive tome.
**Barcelona Walks** by George

Semler; veteran travel journalist leads you through the streets of Barcelona, offering fascinating facts, stories and insights along the way.

**Catalan Cuisine** by Colman Andrews; a senior writer at *American Gourmet* magazine, Andrews's book continues to be the definitive guide to Catalan food culture.

**City of Marvels** by Eduardo Mendoza; a best-selling novel in Spain, this is a tale of corruption, love and intrigue, as well as providing an entertaining insight into Catalan politics of the *fin de siècle*. Beach reading for the thinking man and woman.

**Homage to Catalonia** by George Orwell; the classic Civil War account.

**Shadow of the Wind** by Carlos Ruiz Zafón; like travellers to India clutching their copy of Salman Rushdie's *Midnights Children*, so now visitors to Barcelona come with Zafón's spooky thriller, set mainly in the old quarter.

## Bookshops

**Casa del Llibre**
C/Passeig de Gràcia 62, Eixample; tel: 93 272 3480; www.casadellibro.com; Mon–Sat 9.30am–9.30pm; metro: Passeig de Gràcia; map p.134 B2
A Mecca for book lovers that stocks a good range of Catalan, Spanish and English literature, beach reads and reference books.

**La Central**
C/Elisabets 6, Raval; tel: 93 487 5018; www.lacentral.com; Mon–Fri 9.30am–9.30pm, Sat 10am–9pm; metro: Liceu; map p.138 A4
A highbrow chain that stocks everything from books on history and architecture to study guides and contemporary novels.

**Elephant**
Creu dels Molers 12, Poble Sec; tel: 93 443 0594; www.lfant.biz; daily 10am–8pm; metro: Poble Sec; map p.137 D3
Tucked away in this sleepy *barrio*, this rambling store is stuffed floor to ceiling with new and second-hand English-language books. Second-hand editions never cost more than €3.

**Laie Libreria**
C/Pau Claris 85, Eixample; tel: 93 302 73 10; Mon

**Left and below:** Laie Libreria.

8.30am–9pm, Tue–Fri until 1am, Sat 10am–1am; www.laie.es; metro: Urquinoana; map p.134 B1
This classic bookshop-cum-coffee shop has the atmosphere of a New York Barnes & Noble, but the altogether more satisfying look of old Europe with its sturdy wood shelves and aged tiled floors. Occasional poetry and jazz nights are a hub for the city's bohemians.

**La Llibreria del Sol I de Luna**
C/Canuda 24, Barri Gòtic; no phone; Tue–Sat 10am–1.30pm, 5–8.30pm; metro: Catalunya; map p.138 B4
A delightful bookstore dating back to 1766, with a fine selection of antique tomes. Check out the plaque at the bottom of the door that reads: *El Llibre Fa Lliure* – books make you free.

**Llibreria de la Generalitat**
La Rambla 118; tel: 93 302 6462; Mon–Fri 8am–9pm, Sat 9am–2pm, 4–8pm; metro: Liceu; map p.138 B4
A one-stop shop for guidebooks, glossy coffee-table tomes and maps specific to the region.

# Markets

Barcelona markets are full of promise, mainly of the edible variety. With 40 *barrios*, and one fresh-produce market for each, think picnics and market-stall grazing. Many of the city's *plaças* also spill over on certain days of the month, with market stalls selling everything from mountain honey to bric-a-brac and local crafts. A good time of year to visit is Christmas, when you will find a quirkily festive atmosphere: where else could you find a Christmas crapper *(see box)* to add to your Nativity scene? If you're mad for markets www.mercatsbcn.com gives a full overview. For food shops, *see Food and Drink, p.54–7*.

## La Boqueria
La Rambla 98, La Rambla; tel: 93 423 4287; www.boqueria.info; Mon–Sat 8am–8.30pm; metro: Liceu; map p.138 A3

The most impressive and the most beautiful of Barcelona's many markets, La Boqueria is up there with the Sagrada Família when it comes to must-see sights. Because of this it can also be besieged by camera-toting tourists, so it is best to visit early and avoid Saturdays. That said, it is a paradise for food lovers, with new and more exciting things on offer every day. But if you are the kind of traveller who likes to discover something new, head to other neighbourhoods for a more local flavour.

## Els Encants
C/Dos de Maig 177–187, Eixample; tel: 93 246 3030; www.encantsbcn.com; Mon, Wed, Fri, Sat 9am–2pm; metro: Glòries; map p.135 E1

If you are the kind of traveller that enjoys scavenging for a bargain, Els Encants won't disappoint. It is one of the oldest markets in Europe, dating back to the 14th century, and it is the only market in Barcelona that reflects the Parisian-style flea markets of the 19th century. There is an awful lot of rubbish here, but those prepared to root around will be rewarded with flamenco dresses, good-quality leather and sheepskin coats and vintage furniture. Antiques auctions start at 7am, with sell-offs at noon.

## Fira Artesana
Plaça del Pi s/n, Barri Gòtic; first Fri and Sat of month; metro: Liceu; map p.138 B3

Good for slow-food enthusiasts, this medieval-style market offers a good selection of local goodies. Look out for sausage from Pallars, goat's cheese from Montanya and chocolate from the witches of Cervera.

## Mercat Barceloneta
Plaça Font 1, Barceloneta; tel: 93 221 6471; Mon 7am–3pm, Tue–Thur 7am–3pm, 5–8.30pm, Fri 7am–8.30pm, Sat 7am–3pm; metro: Barceloneta; map p.138 C1

Something of a dud at least when it comes to aesthetics, the prison-grey exterior and barren plaça in front make this a bit of a disappointment after so many years in the making. Given the neighbour-

**Left:** Mercat de Santa Caterina.

**Left:** fresh fruit at the bustling La Boqueria market.

7.30am–3.30pm; metro: Jaume I; map p.138 C3

The late Enric Miralles's *(see box, p.26)* exuberant contribution to the cityscape is a dream-coat of colour. The undulating roof's many hues were conceived to reflect the produce within, while the aisles and stalls seem spacious and bright thanks to a timber-beamed roof that lets light flood in. The shopping here is good, too, like the surroundings, a civilised experience compared to the jostling and elbowing of the Boqueria, with some interesting stalls such as Olisolivo, which has hundreds of bottles of small-production olive oil.

**Mon Raval**

Rambla del Raval s/n, Raval; Sat–Sun 11am–5pm (approx); metro: Sant Antoni, Paral·lel or Liceu; map p.138 A3

This hip little market that runs the length of Rambla del Raval at weekends has a distinctly Moroccan feel. Stalls comprise some good-quality if quirky clothing by design students, bags and accessories. Moroccan food stands serving baklava and sweet mint tea lend a festive air. Note: if there are other community activities such as festivals or music on the Rambla, it doesn't open.

**Seasonal fairs:** The feast of **Sant Jordi** is commemorated with books and roses on 23 April, taking place mainly around the Ramblas. Soon after comes the bewitching street market of **Sant Ponç** on the C/Hospital, with stalls laden with preserves and honey, herbs and medicinal plants. In the autumn the **Mostra de Vins i Caves** takes place on the Moll d'Espanya, where local wine and cava makers come to showcase their wares. At the start of December the annual **Santa Llúcia fair** sets up in front of the cathedral. Dating back hundreds of years, it sells traditional Christmas decorations, including the notorious *caganer*, an explicit rendition of a person taking a dump.

**Mercat de Sant Antoni**

C/Comte d'Urgell 1, Sant Antoni; tel: 93 423 4287; Mon–Thur, Sat 7am–2.30pm, 5.30–8.30pm, Fri 7.30am–8.30pm; metro: Sant Antoni; map p.137 D4

This wonderful Modernista market is up for renovation in 2008, and works are estimated to take about three years, but the plans look promising. Four legs spin off from an ornately decorated, crown-shaped heart, which give it a maze-like quality. A clothing market currently encircles the outside, but this will be replaced by wide-planted plaças between each leg for the more serious business of eating and drinking. On Sunday a popular second-hand books, vintage magazines (lots of mad 1970s porn) and coins market draws crowds from far and wide.

**Mercat de Santa Caterina**

Avda Francesc Cambó 16, Born; tel: 93 319 5740; www.mercat santacaterina.net; Mon 7.30am–2pm, Tue, Wed 7.30am–3.30pm, Thur, Fri 7.30am–8.30pm, Sat

hood, you'd expect a certain screeching fishwife atmosphere, but the days when fishermen bought their haul in here are long gone. Even the trendy bars that encircle it fail to live up to expectations, with one notable exception: El Restaurant Lluçanès, in the eaves of the building, which recently got a Michelin star.

**Right:** furniture at Els Encants.

# Modernisme

At the turn of the last century Art Nouveau had swept across Europe, and in Catalonia had coincided with a period of economic growth that allowed Modernisme, the local version of it, to flourish. Wealthy merchants were buying vast properties, particularly in the Eixample, and commissioning architects such as Antoni Gaudí (1852–1926), Lluis Domènech i Montaner (1850–1923) and Josep Puig i Cadafalch (1867–1956) to remodel them in fabulously ornate ways. Modernisme comprised more than architecture, however, and other notable names include artists Santiago Rusiñol and Ramon Casas.

## Barri Gòtic

### Els Quatre Gats

C/Montsió 3; tel: 93 302 4140; www.4gats.com; daily 8am–2am; metro: Catalunya; map p.138 B4

A bar/restaurant frequented by a young Picasso and other artists of the time at the turn of the last century. The building was one of the first commissions of **Puig i Cadafalch**, and the exquisitely tiled interior is typical of his geometric, polychrome style. The brick façade has Gothic touches and features carvings by Eusebi Arnau, along with a statue of George and the dragon – also a trademark feature of Puig's work.

## Sant Pere and Born

### Palau de la Música Catalana

C/Sant Francesc de Paula 2; tel: 93 295 7200; www.palau musica.org; guided tours daily 10am–3.30pm, until 6pm Aug; admission charge; metro: Urquinaona; map p.138 B4

An extravaganza of a concert hall designed by **Domènech i Montaner** in 1908, and declared a World Heritage Site by Unesco. The only concert hall in Europe to be naturally lit, its interior is a riot of stained glass and floral ceramics. The stage itself has a magnificent mosaic backdrop of musical muses, and is flanked by gravity-defying stone sculptures that include a bust of Beethoven and a surging mass of Valkyries apparently riding out into mid-air. The exterior is no less exuberant, with kaleidoscopic tiling and mosaics and a frothy stone sculpture representing an allegory of popular music.

Tours are informative, but perhaps the best way to see the building is to attend a concert (check website for details of performances).

## Raval

### Hotel España

C/Sant Pau 9–11; tel: 93 318 1758; www.hotelespanya.com; metro: Liceu; map p.138 A3

Not a Modernista building per se, the Hotel España has dining rooms remodelled by **Domènech i Montaner**, worth visiting for their woodwork and colourful tiling. There are fine aquatic murals by artist **Ramon Casas**, along with an intricately sculpted fireplace by **Eusebi Arnau**.

SEE ALSO HOTELS, P.67

**Left:** El Quatre Gats.

The *Ruta del Modernisme* is a guidebook (12 euros) available from the Plaça de Catalunya tourist office that gives discounts and information on many of Barcelona's most important Modernista buildings. For details, *see* www.rutadel modernisme.com.

## Palau Güell

C/Nou de la Rambla 3–5; tel: 93 317 3974; www.palauguell.cat; Tue–Sat 10am–2.30pm; free; metro: Liceu; map p.138 A3
Lengthy renovation work has meant that Palau Güell has been closed to the public for several years, but it was recently decided to open the ground floor and subterranean stables, with a 'virtual visit' screened within. The mansion was built by **Antoni Gaudí** between 1885 and 1889 as the home of his patron, Eusebi Güell. It's a slightly sinister-looking medievalist structure, where Gothic inspiration alternates with evidence of Arabic influence. The building is structured around an enormous salon, from which a conical roof covered in pieces of tiling emerges to preside over an unusual landscape of capriciously placed

**Left and below:** Domènech i Montaner's exquisite Palau de la Música Catalana.

battlements, balustrades and strangely shaped chimneys.

## The Eixample

### Casa Amatller

Passeig de Gràcia 41; metro: Passeig de Gràcia; map p.134 B2
Built by **Puig i Cadafalch** for chocolate-maker Antoni Amatller, the Casa Amatller is a stepped neo-Gothic fantasy, rendered more sober by its neighbour the Casa Batlló. Sadly the interior can't be visited, but the façade is the apotheosis of Puig's style, showing Flemish influences in its colourful geometric tiling, but with traditional touches such as Eusebi Arnau's sculpture of George and the dragon. Some of its original furniture is on show at the MNAC (*see p.90*).

### Casa Batlló

Passeig de Gràcia 43; tel: 93 488 0666; www.casabatllo.cat; daily 9am–8pm; admission charge; metro: Passeig de Gràcia; map p.134 B2
Remodelled by **Gaudí** in 1906, the Casa Batlló is considered the ultimate Gaudí masterpiece. Much of the building is now open to the public, including the main grand floor, the attic and rooftop with its extraordinary

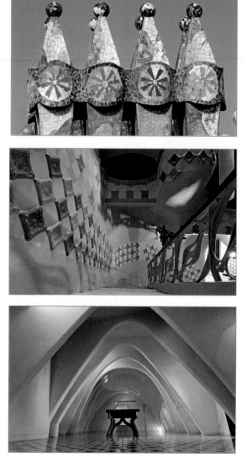

**Left:** Gaudí's Casa Batlló.

Batlló, this one is a frothy confection in stone, often compared to a wedding cake. The façade boasts some spectacular sculptures by Eusebi Arnau, though many were destroyed when Loewe knocked some of the walls out to create their shop windows. The building is closed to the public, but some of its glorious ceramics and mosaic-work can be seen in the entrance round the corner on C/Consell de Cent.

**Hospital Sant Pau**
C/Sant Antoni Maria Claret 167; tel: 93 291 9000; www.sant pau.es; free; metro: Hospital de Sant Pau; map p.135 E4

A short walk up from the Sagrada Família along the Avinguda de Gaudí is the little-visited but hugely rewarding Hospital Sant Pau. Created by the philanthropic **Domènech i Montaner**, who was a great believer in the curative effects of beauty and nature, it comprises a number of extravagantly designed pavilions, each serving as a ward. To retain the idyllic nature of the garden setting, there are subterranean tunnels linking the buildings.

**La Pedrera**
C/Provença 261–265; tel: 93 484 5900; www.caixacatalunya. cat; Mar–Oct: daily 9am–8pm, Nov–Feb: 9am–6.30pm; admission charge; metro: Diagonal, FGC: Provença; map p.134 B3

**Gaudí**'s Casa Milà is more often known as La Pedrera ('The Stone Quarry') because of its rippling grey façade. Like so many of his buildings it was the subject of passionate debate between enthusiasts and denigrators at the time of its construction in 1910. In the

chimneys, while the upper floors are still occupied. Gaudí's remodelling took out all the right angles and added plasterwork apparently sculpted from whipped cream, sinuous window and door frames and a light well tiled with iridescent blues. The façade is a fantastical representation – depending which version you believe – of George slaying the dragon. The humpbacked roof glittering with scale-like tiles repre-

sents the beast itself, the tower George's lance and the skeletal balconies the bones of its victims.

**Casa Lleó Morera**
Passeig de Gràcia 35; metro: Passeig de Gràcia; map p.134 B2

The third jewel of Modernisme on the Manzana de la Discòrdia ('Block of Discord'), as this stretch is known, is **Domènech i Montaner**'s Casa Lleó Morera. Completely different in style from either the Casa Amatller or the Casa

**Right:** the façade of La Pedrera, and the Sagrada Família.

For some examples of Modernista furniture, the **MNAC** *(see p.90)* is worth a visit. Particularly outstanding are the pieces by Gaspar Homar and the huge painting by Ramon Casas of himself and Pere Romeu riding a tandem, a copy of which still sits in Els Quatre Gats *(see p.29, 80)*, once Romeu's bar.

attic is the **Espai Gaudí**, an enlightening exhibition of the architect's work, and **El Pis**, one of the flats now open to the public and decorated as it would have been when the building was first occupied. Above is a spectacular roof, whose chimneys have been dubbed the 'witch scarers'. Major temporary exhibitions are held regularly on the first floor and are open to the public free of charge.
SEE ALSO MUSIC, P.93

### Sagrada Família
C/Mallorca 401; tel: 93 207 3031; www.sagradafamilia.org; summer: daily 9am–8pm, winter: daily 9am–6pm; admission charge; metro: Sagrada Família; map p.135 D2

The Sagrada Família is perhaps **Gaudí**'s best-known work, but was actually begun in 1882 as a neo-Gothic structure under the direction of the architect **Francesc Vil-**

lar, and came under Gaudí's control a year later. He never expected to see its completion, stating: 'It is not possible for one generation to erect the entire temple', but his death in 1926, after he was hit by a tram, meant that he spent rather less time on it than expected.

The building arouses awe and horror almost equally (and was famously hated by George Orwell). Some prefer the sinuous organic forms of Gaudí's Nativity façade, while others prefer the stark strength of **Josep Subirach**'s figures on the modern Passion façade: few share equal enthusiasm for both. It is in the Sagrada Família that Gaudí's obsession with nature took full flight, and every surface drips with stone flora and fauna.
SEE ALSO CHURCHES, P.39

### Upper Neighbourhoods

#### Casa Vicens
C/Carolines 18–24; metro: Fontana

A private residence, built by Gaudí for a tile manufacturer in 1883–8. The house also functioned as an advert for its owner's business, and its spectacular ceramics sit in contrast to the red brick.

#### Park Güell
C/Olot; tel: 93 285 6899; daily:

May–Sept: 10am–9pm, Apr and Oct: 10am–8pm, Mar and Nov: 10am–7pm, Dec–Feb: 10am–6pm; free; metro: Vallcarca

The Park Güell was originally planned as a garden city on the estate of the wealthy industrialist Eusebi Güell, who went on to commission **Gaudí** for several other projects. The estate was to encompass 60 building plots, but only five buildings were completed: the two pavilions flanking the entrance, both designed by Gaudí, and three others inside the park. In creating Park Güell, Gaudí used shapes that harmonised with the landscape. Always aware of the struggle between man and nature, he built a complex garden of staircases, zoomorphic sculptures, sinuous ramps and viaducts.

The most important single element of the park is a two-tiered plaza 86 by 40 metres (280 by 130ft). The lower part, made up of a series of columns in the form of a *sala hipóstila*, was designed to be the market place. The upper portion is an open esplanade with grand views over the city, surrounded by an undulating bench of mosaics, whose detailing is largely the work of master ceramicist **Josep Maria Jujol**.

# Museums and Galleries

The charm of Barcelona's museum scene is a delightfully quirky one. There are no must-see international collections; Catalan pride makes for a diverse and idiosyncratic array, celebrating its most famous sons (Museu Picasso, Fundació Joan Miró, Fundació Antoni Tàpies), its most colourful eccentrics (Museu Frederic Marès) and its favourite indulgence (Chocolate Museum). Others, such as the Museu Marítim, the MACBA and the Museu d'Història de la Ciutat, are worth seeing for their extraordinary buildings alone.

## Barri Gòtic

### Museu del Calçat (Shoe Museum)

Plaça Sant Felip Neri 5; tel: 93 301 4533; Tue–Sun 11am–2pm; admission charge; metro: Jaume I; map p.138 B3

An eccentric collection of footwear going back to medieval times and housed in what was once the head-quarters of the Shoemakers' Guild. The building used to be in a street opposite the cathedral (see p.38) – since cleared to make Avinguda de la Catedral – and was moved to this tiny plaça, brick by brick. An enormous shoe made to measure for the Columbus statue in La Rambla and a gold stiletto worn by Catalan soprano Victoria de los Ángeles are among the curiosities on display.

### Museu Diocesà

Avda Catedral 4; tel: 93 315 2213; Jan–May, Oct–Dec: Tue–Sat 10am–2pm, 5–8pm, Sun 11am–2pm, 5–8pm, June–Sept: daily 10am–8pm; admission charge; metro: Jaume I; map p.138 B3

This simple, elegant Gothic building was once an almshouse, where 100 meals were given to the poor daily. It now houses the Museu Diocesà, with a small but varied collection of religious art and statuary and Romanesque murals. It also holds hit-or-miss temporary exhibitions on mostly Mediterranean artists.

Until recently the **MACBA** (see p.87) was almost alone in opening on a Monday, leaving tourists with little to do, but Barcelona's two newest museums – the **Museu de la Música** (see p.91) and the **Museu Olímpic** (see p.90), both have Tuesday as their closing day. In early 2008 **CaixaForum** (see p.89) announced it was to stay open every day.

**Left:** Richard Meier's gleaming white MACBA.

The **Arqueoticket** is a new ticket costing €17 and giving admission to the Museu d'Arqueologia *(see p.90)*, Museu Barbier-Mueller *(see below)*, Museu Egipci, Museu d'Història de la Ciutat *(see below)* and the Museu Marítim *(see p.88)*. It's available from tourist offices and from the museums themselves.

Right column text:

wall as its north side. The decorated ceiling timbers are by Alfonso de Córdoba and the beautiful Epiphany altarpiece painted by Jaume Huguet in 1465. It also houses the stone on which the saint's breasts were mutilated.

To the other side is the **Torre de Martí I**, sometimes called a mirador because of its views over the city, though it is closed to the public indefinitely. The tower was built by Antoni Carbonell and is named after Martí I ('the Humanist', 1396–1410), last in the 500-year dynasty of Barcelona count-kings.

### Sant Pere and Born

**Museu Barbier-Mueller d'Art Precolombí**
C/Montcada 12–14; tel: 93 310 4516; www.barbier-mueller.ch; Tue–Fri 11am–7pm, Sat 10am–7pm, Sun 10am–3pm; admission charge; metro: Jaume I; map p.138 C3
A small but prestigious collection of pre-Columbian art and artefacts, representing most styles of pre-Hispanic

**Barcelona's Best Museums for Art**
MNAC *(see p.90)*
Fundació Joan Miró *(see p.89)*
Museu Picasso *(see p.86)*
CaixaForum *(see p.89)*

### Museu Frederic Marès
Plaça de Sant Iu 5–6; tel: 93 310 5800; www.museumares.bcn. cat; Tue–Sat 10am–7pm, Sun 10am–3pm; admission charge; metro: Jaume I; map p.138 B3
This quirky assortment, donated by Catalan sculptor Marès in 1946, is one of the most interesting in the city. As well as some of his own work, and that of other Catalan and Spanish sculptors, the building houses a hotchpotch of items, from an extraordinary collection of Romanesque crucifixes in the basement to a pretty array of ladies' fans and a whole floor of antique toys.

### Museu d'Història de la Ciutat
Plaça del Rei s/n; tel: 93 256 2100; www.museuhistoria.bcn. cat; Oct–Mar: Tue–Sat 10am–2pm, 4–7pm, Sun 10am–3pm; Apr–Sept: Tue–Sat 10am–8pm, Sun till 3pm; admission charge; metro: Jaume I; map p.138 B3
The main attraction of the City History Museum are the excavations of the Roman city that flourished between the 1st and 7th centuries. Covering

**Left:** Museu Frederic Marès.

4,000 sq metres (43,000 sq ft) beneath the Plaça del Rei, the remains offer an intriguing insight not only into Roman building methods, but also into commercial and domestic life. The museum's eclectic collection, not all on show, also includes maps, models, Roman portraits, guild paraphernalia and an anarchist's bomb that damaged the Liceu in 1893.

The museum is also worth a visit, however, for the buildings in which it is housed. Once forming the Royal Palace complex, they include the great **Saló del Tinell**, one of the finest examples of Catalan Gothic, built in 1359, its six arches spanning an unprecedented 15 metres (50ft). In the 15th century the Inquisition held court in the Saló del Tinell. Legend has it that the tribunal walls cannot bear a lie to be told, and that if this occurred, the ceiling stones would move, adding further to the victims' terror. Today, the salon is an exhibition area.

Next door is the **chapel of Santa Agata**, built for Jaume II (1302–12) using the Roman

American civilisations, and bequeathed to Barcelona by the Geneva Museum. The gift shop has some beautiful contemporary Indian work, albeit at Western prices.

## Museu de Ciències Naturals de la Ciutadella

Parc de la Ciutadella; tel: 93 319 6912; www.bcn.cat/museuciencies; Tue–Sat 10am–6.30pm, Sun 10am–2.30pm; admission charge; metro: Jaume I/Arc de Triomf; map p.139 C3

The Natural History Museum is in fact two museums on a joint ticket; the **Zoological Museum**, housed in the handsome Castell dels Tres Dragons (Castle of the Three Dragons) at the entrance to the park, and the **Geology Museum**, halfway down its southern flank. Both museums have a certain musty, old-world charm, their respective displays of stuffed animals and rows of rocks and fossils sitting rather forlornly in glass cases.

## Museu Picasso

C/Montcada 15–23; tel: 93 256 3000; www.museupicasso. bcn.cat; Tue–Sun 10am–8pm; admission charge; metro: Jaume I; map p.138 C3

The Museu Picasso opened in 1963 as a result of generous donations from Picasso's friend and secretary Jaume Sabartés, and now occupies

Barcelona's Best Museums for Science
CosmoCaixa *(see p.91)*
Museu de Ciències *(see left)*

five medieval mansions along the Carrer Montcada: **Palau Berenguer d'Aguilar**, **Baró de Castellet**, **Meca**, **Casa Mauri** and **Finestres**. The last two, opened in October 1999, are for the often fascinating temporary exhibitions; the main entrance is through the 15th-century Aguilar palace. Its beautiful courtyard, with a surrounding first-floor gallery and pointed archways resting on slender columns, was designed by Marc Safont, who is best-known for the inner patio of the Generalitat building.

The museum has the most complete collection of Picasso's early works, mostly those dating from his formative years in Barcelona (where his father was an art teacher), including sketches in schoolbooks and a masterly portrait of his mother, done when he was only 16 years old. Other early masterpieces include *First Communion* and *Science and Charity*. The Blue Period (1901–4) is especially well represented. It is an absorbing collection, although there are only a limited number of Picasso's later works, apart

**Right:** modern art exhibits at the MACBA.

from the fascinating cubist studies of Velázquez's *Las Meninas* dating from the 1950s, and some lesser-known but absorbing ceramic pieces.

## Museu de la Xocolata (Chocolate Museum)

C/Comerç 36; tel: 93 268 7878; www.pastisseria.cat; Mon, Wed–Sat 10am–7pm, Sun 10am–3pm; admission charge; metro: Jaume I; map p.139 C3

Barcelona prides itself on a connoisseurship of chocolate, something mostly clearly demonstrated here, with a whole museum dedicated to the brown stuff. Various exhibits illustrate 'a route through the origins of chocolate', but the best-loved pieces on show are the *mones* – vast and elaborate chocolate sculptures of Barcelona landmarks, popular figures and so on.

## Raval

### CCCB (Centre de Cultura Contemporània de Barcelona)

C/Montalegre 5; tel: 93 306 4100; www.cccb.org; Tue–Sun 11am–8pm, Thur 11am–10pm; admission charge; metro: Catalunya/Universitat; map p.138 A4

This former 18th-century hospice once formed part of the enormous Casa de la Caritat (almshouse), which provided a home for thousands of children. More recently it was transformed into the CCCB, a series of spaces for diverse cultural activities, including exhibitions and festivals of art, dance, music, film and video, among other things. The complex – a wonderful reno-

**Left:** exhibits at Museu Barbier-Mueller d'Art Precolombí.

vation by prestigious architects Piñón and Vilaplana –
rivals the MACBA *(see right)*
for its architectural interest.

The C3 Bar, with a terrace
overlooking the quiet square
at the back, is a good place
to meet and snack, convert-
ing into a candlelit outdoor
lounge bar at night.

**Centre d'Art Santa Mònica**
La Rambla 7; tel: 93 316 2810;
www.centredartsantamonica.net;
Tue–Sat 11am–8pm, Sun
11am–3pm; free; metro: Drassanes; map p.138 A2
A sleek exhibition hall run by
the Generalitat and housed in
a former 17th-century

convent. Twenty exhibitions
a year bring together local
and international artists,
while the first floor is dedicated to art education and
activities, open to the public.

The La Central gift shop in the
**MACBA** complex *(see right)* is
a wonderful place to pick up
stylish souvenirs, from designer
t-shirts to retro fridge magnets
and coffee-table books about
the city. It is open Oct–June:
Wed–Mon 10.30am–8pm, Sun
10.30am–3pm and July–Sept:
Wed–Mon 10.30am–8.30pm,
Sun 10.30am–3pm.

A pleasant terrace café overlooks La Rambla.

**MACBA**
**(Museu d'Art Contem-
porani de Barcelona)**
Plaça dels Àngels 1; tel: 93 412
0810; www.macba.es; June–
Sept: Mon, Wed, Thur 11am–8pm,
Fri, Sat 11am–midnight, Sun
10am–3pm, Oct–May: Mon, Wed–
Fri 11am–7.30pm, Sat 10am–
8pm, Sun 10am–3pm; admission
charge; metro: Catalunya/Univer-
sitat; map p.138 A4
Designed by US architect
Richard Meier and opened in
1995, the white MACBA
building is dazzling against
the blue Mediterranean sky

and gigantic within the context of the humble buildings beyond. The social and urban significance of the architecture in this once declining area has often been more of a talking point than the works inside, which comprise Catalan, Spanish and some international art from the last 50 years. The collection is not intended to be an overview, but focuses on certain defining movements of the last few decades. The museum also hosts interesting temporary exhibitions.

Its large forecourt, with a solid bronze sculpture by **Jorge Oteiza** and a mural by fellow Basque **Eduardo Chillida**, has evolved into a popular public space for skateboarding and football matches.

### Museu Marítim
Avda Drassanes s/n; tel: 93 342 9920; www.museumaritim barcelona.com; daily 10am–7pm; admission charge; metro: Drassanes; map p.138 A2
One of the most imposing

On the roof of the **Museu d'Història de Catalunya** *(see below)* is a café-restaurant with great views over the port and Barcelona skyline from its terrace. It has the same opening hours as the museum and serves a decent *menú* (fixed-price lunch).

aspects of the Maritime Museum is the building itself – the magnificent Gothic former shipyards dating from the 13th century are a fine and rare example of civil architecture from that period. The collection includes real fishing boats from the Catalan coast and models of vessels from all ages. Also on display is a modern Olympic winner, maps, instruments and paintings. The highlight, however, is the full-scale replica of the 16th-century galley in which Don Juan of Austria led the Christian fleet to defeat the Turks in the battle of Lepanto in 1571. Also

included in the ticket is a visit to the **Santa Eulàlia**, an old sailing boat which was once used to carry cargo to the Americas and is now moored in the port nearby.

### The Waterfront and Poblenou
### Museu d'Història de Catalunya
Plaça de Pau Vila 3; tel: 93 225 4700; www.mhcat.net; Tue–Sat 10am–7pm, Wed 10am–8pm, Sun 10am–2.30pm; admission charge; metro: Barceloneta; map p.138 C2
In 1992 a former warehouse complex, the Magatzem General de Comerç (1878) by Elias Rogent, was transformed into the **Palau de Mar**. The building has been very well renovated, and part of it now houses the fascinating Catalan History Museum. True to its name, it elucidates Catalan history, but also serves as a generic history museum with various bits of technical wizardry and plenty

of interactive spaces – try walking in a suit of armour, or building a Roman arch – which kids of all ages love.

## Montjuïc, Poble Sec and Sant Antoni

### CaixaForum

Casaramona, Avda Marquès de Comillas 6–8; tel: 93 476 8600; www.fundacio.lacaixa.es; Sun–Fri 10am–8pm, Sat 10am–10pm; free; metro: Espanya; map p.136 B4

The Casaramona is a fascinating former textile factory built by Puig i Cadafalch in 1911. A gem of Modernista industrial architecture, it was overlooked for years but finally rescued by the wealthy Fundació La Caixa, which converted it into their new cultural centre, the CaixaForum. It is a wonderful space, with a subterranean entrance designed by **Arata Isozaki** and a wildly colourful mural by **Sol Lewitt** in the foyer. Apart from its own small contemporary art collection, it puts on some of the best temporary exhibitions in the city, concerts, debates and festivals.

### Fundació Fran Daurel

Poble Espanyol, Avda Marquès de Comillas; tel: 93 423 4172; www.fundaciofrandaurel.com; daily 10am–7pm; admission charge; metro: Espanya; map p.136 B4

A compact collection of contemporary art, most of it Spanish. Alongside a handful of sketches, lithographs and ceramics by **Miró**, **Dalí** and **Picasso**, are dozens more by the most influential Spanish artists of the moment, such as **Antoni Tàpies** or **Perejaume**. There is also a sculpture garden.

### Fundació Joan Miró

Parc de Montjuïc s/n; tel: 93 443 9470; www.bcn.fjmiro.cat; Oct–June: Tue–Sat 10am–7pm, Thur until 9.30pm, Sun until 2.30pm, July–Sept: Tue–Sun until 8pm, Thur until 9.30pm, Sun until 2.30pm; admission charge; metro: Paral·lel and funicular; map p.136 C2

Designed by **Josep Lluis Sert**, eminent architect and friend of **Miró**, this gallery has been open since 1974. Its gleaming luminosity reminiscent of Miró's home and studio in Palma de Mallorca, the striking building shows his work in the best possible light. One of the largest Miró collections, it includes paintings, drawings, sculptures and tapestries, as well as his complete graphic work. It also contains the mercury fountain designed by **Alexander Calder** for the Spanish

*Left and above:* stars of the sea at the Museu Marítim.

Republic's pavilion in the 1937 Paris Exhibition, and hosts some of the best temporary exhibitions in the city.

## MNAC (Museu Nacional d'Art de Catalunya)

Palau Nacional; tel: 93 622 0376; www.mnac.cat; Tue–Sat 10am–7pm, Sun 10am–2.30pm; admission charge; metro: Espanya; map p.136 B3

While visitor numbers are nowhere near those for the Museu Picasso (see p.86) or even the Nou Camp tour (see p.118), many would argue that this is Barcelona's most fascinating museum. It houses the most important Romanesque art collection in the world, including murals that were peeled from the walls of tiny churches in the Pyrenees in the province of Lleida and brought down by donkey. There is also an excellent Gothic collection and a small but growing selection of Renaissance and baroque art.

The building has undergone major renovation work over the last decade under the direction of the Italian architect **Gae Aulenti**, but reopened to show a millennium of Catalan art. The original collection has been complemented by the 19th- and 20th-century Modernista works from the former Museu d'Art Modern, which includes work by **Casas**, **Rusiñol**, **Nonell** and **Fortuny**, and the decorative arts, including pieces by **Gaudí** and **Jujol**. The museum now also houses the small but notable **Thyssen** collection of paintings, formerly in the Monestir de Pedralbes.

## Museu d'Arqueologia de Catalunya

Passeig de Santa Madrona 39–41; tel: 93 424 6577; www.mac.cat; Tue–Sat 9.30am–7pm, Sun 10am–2.30pm; admission charge; metro: Espanya/Poble Sec; map p.136 C3

Catalonia's national archaeology museum contains interesting discoveries from the prehistoric inhabitants of Catalonia up until medieval times, but most notably from the Greek and Roman periods. Temporary exhibitions have ranged from ancient sculpture to comic-book art.

## Museu Etnològic

Passeig Santa Madrona 16–22; tel: 93 424 6807; www.museuetnologic.cat; Oct–June: Tue, Thur 10am–7pm, Wed, Fri–Sun 10am–2pm, July–Sept: Tue, Thur, Fri noon–8pm, Sun 11am–3pm; admission charge; metro: Poble Sec; map p.136 C3

The Ethnology Museum has collections from all over the world, notably Latin America and the Philippines. A section on Japan, the Espai Japó, is an indication of the new cultural exchange between Catalonia and Japan.

## Museu Militar

Castell de Montjuïc, Ctra de Montjuïc 66; tel: 93 329 8613; www.museomilitarmontjuic.es; Mar–mid-Nov: Tue–Fri 9.30am–7pm, Sat–Sun 9.30am–8pm, mid-Nov–Feb: Tue–Fri 9.30am–5pm, Sat–Sun 9.30am–7pm (hours may vary); admission charge; metro: Paral·lel and funicular; map p.136 C1

Montjuïc's castle has little appeal for Catalans, as it represents hated oppression from the central government in Madrid, and is a place where torture and executions took place over many years. Today the castle houses the Military Museum, with a collection of weapons, lead soldiers and military uniforms, but there are plans to convert it into a Centre for Peace, as the Spanish government has ceded its ownership to Catalonia.

## Museu Olímpic i de l'Esport

Avda Estadi 60; tel: 93 292 5379; Apr–Sept: Mon, Wed–Sun 10am–8pm, Oct–Mar: Mon, Wed–Sun 10am–6pm; admission charge; metro: Espanya/Paral·lel and funicular; map p.136 B2

The holdings of the small Galeria Olímpica in the Olympic Stadium were moved in 2007 to this new,

architecturally designed home set into the hill nearby. While focusing on the Barcelona Olympics in 1992, it gives a global view of the sporting world, with interactive exhibits and multi-media installations.

## The Eixample

### Fundació Antoni Tàpies

C/Aragó 255; tel: 93 487 0315; www.fundaciotapies.org; Tue–Sun 10am–8pm; admission charge; metro: Passeig de Gràcia/Catalunya; map p.134 B2

Reputedly the first Modernista building, this was built by Domènech i Montaner in 1886 for publishers Montaner i Simón, and in 1990 became the setting for the large collection of work by Antoni Tàpies, who is considered to be Spain's greatest living artist. It is closed until July 2008, at the earliest, for renovations, but is still worth visiting for one of his more ethereal sculptures, *Núvol i Cadira* (Cloud and Chair), which floats atop the building.

### Fundació Suñol

Passeig de Gràcia 98; tel: 93 496 1032; www.fundaciosunol.org; Mon–Wed, Fri–Sat 4–8pm; admission charge; metro: Diagonal; map p.134 B3

The important private collection of Josep Suñol was made public in 2007 in a series of spaces that include terraces for sculptures and

**Left:** Fundació Joan Miró.

the Nivell Zero, an exhibition hall dedicated to young Spanish artists. The 1,200 works of art of the permanent collection are rotated on a six-monthly basis, but include contemporary paintings, sculpture and photographs by **Picasso**, **Dalí**, **Miró**, **Giacometti**, **Man Ray** and **Andy Warhol**.

### Museu de la Música

L'Auditori, C/Padilla 155 2ª; tel: 93 256 3650; www.museumusica.bcn.cat; Mon, Wed–Fri 11am–9pm, Sat–Sun 10am–7pm; admission charge; metro: Glòries; map p.135 E1

Newly opened in 2007 within the complex of the **Auditori** concert halls *(see p.92)*, the Music Museum is actually a rehousing of a collection that has been under wraps for several years while a suitable venue was sought. Instruments from different eras are sumptuously displayed in dramatically spotlit glass cases amid red carpeting, while the interactive section provides budding rock stars with the opportunity to let rip.

## Upper Neighbourhoods

### CosmoCaixa

C/Teodor Roviralta 47–51, Tibidabo; tel: 93 212 6050; www.fundaciolacaixa.es; Tue–Sun 10am–8pm; admission charge; FGC: Avda Tibidabo

CosmoCaixa is officially Europe's largest science museum, although this is slightly misleading, as much of its space is given over to offices and conference facilities. It has plenty of hands-on exhibits and interesting temporary exhibitions for all ages – the under-7s are catered for in the 'Clik', a space to play and learn created by the high-profile designer Javier

Mariscal, while slightly older children can learn scientific principles through games in the 'Flash' section. Among the other highlights is the **Flooded Forest**, a recreation of part of the Amazon rainforest.

### Museu de Ceràmica/ Museu de les Arts Decoratives

Palau Reial de Pedralbes, Avda Diagonal 686, Pedralbes; tel: (Ceràmica) 93 280 1621 (Arts Decoratives) 93 280 5024; Tue–Sat 10am–6pm, Sun 10am–3pm; admission charge; metro: Palau Reial

The Royal Palace is the result of a 1919 conversion of the antique Can Feliu into a residence for King Alfonso XIII. It is elegant, and the classical garden peaceful, but has little sense of history. The main building cannot be visited, apart from the two museums it houses. The **Museu de Ceràmica** shows the history of Spanish pottery from the 12th century, and has some interesting 20th-century pieces from **Artigas**, **Miró** and **Picasso**. The **Museu de les Arts Decoratives** shows the development of craft techniques from medieval times to the present day, ending with Spain's only industrial-design collection. From July 2008, the contents of the former Textile and Clothing Museum in the Born will also be housed here, and will form part of the same ticket. The three will be known collectively as the **Museu de les Arts Aplicades**.

Since 1977, Barcelona – along with dozens of other cities around the world – has celebrated **International Museum Day** on 18 May. On this day all municipal and some private museums waive their entrance fees, and many lay on live music and other events.

Museums and Galleries

91

# Music

L ive music is an essential part of Barcelona life, though this is not immediately obvious. The climate means that many of the live performances take place on the streets, whether it is annual festivals in the plaças of the Barri Gòtic or buskers livening up the café terraces. With a couple of notable exceptions, it is less common to see live music in the city's bars, and when it comes to seeing bands at the bigger venues expect to pay upwards of €15. This chapter lists the key venues for live music; check the local press or www.barcelonarocks.com to find out what is on during your visit. *See also Festivals, p.48–51.*

## Classical

### L'Auditori

C/Lepant 150; tel: 93 247 9300/93 326 2945 (box office); www.auditori.com; box office: Mon–Sat noon–9pm, Sun 1hr before performance; metro: Glòries; map p.139 E4

Generally (though not exclusively) orientated to more formal presentations by national orchestras and classical interpretations.

### Gran Teatre del Liceu

La Rambla 51–59; tel: 93 485 9913; www.liceubarcelona.com; Mon–Fri 11am–2pm, 3–8pm (general information), Mon–Fri 2–8pm, Sat–Sun 1hr before

> **Free festivals:** year-round music is there for the taking if you time it right. **Festival Guitarra** from April to June; **De Cajón** for flamenco, June–July; **Clàssics als Parcs** for classical music on a patch of green.
>
> **Festival de Tardor Ribermúsica** in the Born in October has an authentic festival spirit. www.barcelonarocks.com is a good all-round guide to what's on when. For more information *see Festivals, p.48–51.*

performance (box office); metro: Liceu; map p.138 A3

One of the most sophisticated opera houses in Europe; the city's citizens are lucky to have it after a fire all but destroyed it in the 1980s. The original features have been meticulously restored to create a satisfyingly plush experience of red velvet chairs and lashings of gilt. Performances are high-class, with digital subtitles shown on screens inserted into seat backs.

### Palau de la Música Catalana

C/Sant Francesc de Paula 2, Sant Pere; tel: 93 295 7200;

**Left:** the Gran Teatre del Liceu.

www.palaumusica.org; Mon–Sat 10am–9pm, Sun 1 hr before performance (box office); metro: Uruinaona; map p.138 B4

The jewel in Barcelona's Modernisme crown, the Palau is a lavishly decorated concert hall by Lluís Domènech i Montaner. Intricate mosaic and stained-glass work on the outside are second only to the opulent splendour within. It is worth the price of a ticket to anything just to get the full experience.

SEE ALSO MODERNISME, P.80

## Contemporary

### Razzmatazz

C/Almogàvers 122, Poblenou; tel: 93 320 8200; www.salarazzmatazz.com; Fri–Sat 1am–5am (club nights), see website for upcoming bands; metro: Bogatell or Marina; map p.139 E4

The mothership for big bands, with a leaning towards indie crooners, rock gods or divas from the 1980s. It also doubles as a mega club, which comes in useful. This place can be

**Left:** live music at Harlem Jazz Club.

**Església Santa Maria del Pi** hosts classical Spanish guitar concerts most Fridays and Saturdays. **Santa Maria del Mar** *(see p.38)* has a choral rendition of Handel's *Messiah* at Christmas time.

hellish to get home from once the metro stops running.
SEE ALSO NIGHTLIFE, P.95

**Ribborn**
C/Antic Sant Joan 3, Born; tel: 93 310 7148; www.ribborn.com; Mon–Sun 10am–3am; metro: Barceloneta; map p.138 C3
This seductive little bar with red walls, velvet drapes and stand-up piano by the bar is host to some of the city's best music nights by local performers. Genres change all the time, and range from jazz, funk and soul to reggae; it is a particularly civilised end to the weekend.

## Jazz and Cabaret

**Harlem Jazz Club**
C/Comtessa de Sobradiel 8, Barri Gòtic; tel: 93 310 0755; Tue–Thur, Sun 8pm–4am, Fri–Sat 8pm–5am; metro: Jaume I; map p.138 B3

Dark, smoky and invariably packed to the gills, this is everything a jazz club should be. A varied repertoire of local and bigger-name bands keep things interesting.

**Jamboree**
Plaça Reial 17; tel: 93 319 1789; www.masimas.com; Mon–Sun 9–11pm (live music), midnight–5am (disco); admission charge: €9; metro: Liceu; map p.138 B3
One of the earliest clubs to open on Plaça Reial, which now crawls with them, the dungeonesque Jamboree can be all things to all people. At its best it's a low-key, formally laid out live basement jazz venue (chairs come out to seat aficionados) attracting big-name jazz, blues and folk artists. Chet Baker and Ella Fitzgerald both crooned here in the 1960s, and its reputation as one of the best in Spain endures. After midnight the music pumps out the genre's contemporary versions: acid jazz, bossa nova and chill-out. Upstairs, sister

**Right:** you can buy sheet music at Casa Beethoven; Rambla de Sant Josep 97; tel: 93 301 4826.

venue **Los Tarantos** *(see p.125)* hosts live flamenco performances which are a cut above the average tourist fare.

**La Pedrera del Nit**
Passeig de Gràcia 92, Eixample; tel: 902 400 973; www.caixa catalunya.es; Fri–Sat 9–11.30pm; metro: Diagonal; map p.134 B2
To spend Friday or Saturday night among the 'witch scarers' on Gaudí's rooftop sipping cava and listening to jazz is one of the city's greatest treats. Book at least a week in advance to stand a hope of getting in. Summer only.
SEE ALSO MODERNISME, P.82

**Pastís**
C/Santa Mònica 4, Raval; tel: 93 318 7980; Tue–Thur, Sun 7.30pm–2.30am, Fri–Sat 7.30pm–3.30am, live music Wed; metro: Drassanes; map p.138 A2
Possibly the smallest bar in Barcelona – five people and you have got a crowd – but it is a delightfully eccentric place overflowing with old photos and the odd papier-mâché curio. A shot of pastis and the mournful French ballads from an Edith Piaf lookalike will transport you to Paris.

# Nightlife

$B$arcelona's reputation as a party city is well established – but the abundance of (mainly British) stag parties belies a unique energy that permeates the nightlife scene. There is a willingness to push design and ambience beyond the usual, and this is reflected in the wide variety of bars and clubs on offer in this city. Barcelona doesn't really get going until at least Thursday and then people rarely go out before 11pm. Bars usually stay open until around 2 or 3am, and as a result, clubs (or *discotecas*) do not become lively much before this. This chapter lists a selection of worthy nightspots. *See also Bars and Cafés, p. 28–35.*

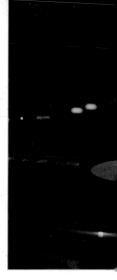

### Barri Gòtic

#### Fonfone
Escudellers 24; tel: 93 317 1424; www.fonfone.com; nightly 11pm–5am; free; metro: Drassenes or Liceu; map p.138 B3
This funky-looking club conveniently located in the centre of everything attracts a mixed crowd of regulars and tourists. Resident DJs play funk, hip-hop and '80s during the week, and the usual mix of electro, house and techno at weekends.

### Sant Pere and Born

#### Club Mix
Comerç 21; tel: 93 319 4696; Tue–Sun 8pm–3am; free before 11pm, then €10; metro: Jaume I; map p.139 C3
Tapas turns into Tanqueray at this upscale, post-work-to-post-dinner lounge club. Near-nightly DJ sessions of rare groove and retro and the high-design interior attract a trendy, Martini-drinking crowd.

#### Diobar
C/Marquès de l'Argentera 27; tel: 93 221 1939; Thur–Sat 11pm–3am; free; metro: Barceloneta; map p.139 C2
It's the playlist of funk and soul sounds that make this bastion of urban cool so popular. Despite its location downstairs from a Greek

restaurant, the abundance of sofas make this club a popular choice for those who prefer their nights lounging rather than dancing.

### Raval

#### Fellini
C/La Rambla 27; tel: 93 272 4980; www.clubfellini.com; Mon–Sat midnight–5am; Mon–Thur free before 1.30am, then €6 before 3am and €9 after, Fri–Sat €9–€12; metro: Liceu; map p.138 A3
Despite its location in the heart of *guiri* territory, Fellini has established itself as one of the most forward-looking clubs in town. The monthly 'Puticlub' is a free-for-all melting pot, and the 'Mond Club' (held on the last Thursday of the month) has achieved almost cult status among the music-savvy crowd.

#### Moog
Arc del Teatre 3; tel: 93 272 0910; www.masimas.com; nightly midnight–5am; admission charge €9; metro: Drassanes; map p.138 A2

**Left:** the Barri Gòtic's bars heave with tourists in summer.

**Left:** noise restrictions haven't stopped the city from partying.

Barcelona mainstay. Featuring closely guarded white beds around the dance floor, Carpe Diem Lounge Club attracts a glittering array of the well endowed (both physically and financially), as well as the odd football player. For those missing the Gold Card, the terrace area provides a funky atmosphere for spotting the latest *¡Hola!* magazine fodder.

### Club Catwalk
C/Ramón Trias Fargas; tel: 93 221 6161; www.clubcatwalk.net; Wed–Sun midnight–5am; admission charge €15–€18; metro: Cuitadella-Vila Olímpica; map p.139 E1

Its location (below the celebrity-magnet Hotel Arts, *see p.68*) means this club attracts a well-heeled, well-dressed crowd up for a night of house tunes (downstairs) or funky R&B (upstairs). Regular appearances by world-famous DJs ensures that the club's reputation is safe.

### Razzmatazz
C/Almogavérs 122 Poblenou; tel: 93 320 8200; www.salarazzmatazz.com; Fri–Sat 1–5am; admission charge varies; metro: Marina or Bogatell; map p.139 E4

Essentially five clubs in one; if you get tired of the techno minimalism of the main room, safe to say you can find an alternative elsewhere upstairs. A wide range of international DJs play here (see the website for current schedules) and, despite the venue being a little run-down and somewhat of a maze to get around, it's always packed with an up-for-it crowd of Converse-wearing party animals.

At 6am, if the mood takes you, there are usually a number of after-parties to tempt you away from sleep for a few hours longer. Ask a suitably 'up-for-it' local for details of the best 'afters'. For a true Barcelona experience, try a night out at some of the smaller, unpretentious local hang-outs. The prices are better, and you can avoid the try-hard fashionistas that populate some of the larger venues.

Resident DJs play house and techo downstairs and '80s upstairs in this small and sweaty mainstay hidden away just off La Rambla.

### The Waterfront and Poblenou

#### Baja Beach
Passeig Marítim 34; tel: 93 225 9100; www.bajabeach.es; June–Oct: Mon–Wed, Sun 11am–midnight, Fri–Sat 11am–6am, Nov–May: Thur–Sat 11am–6am, Sun 11am–midnight; admission charge Wed €10, Thur, Sun €12, Fri €14, Sat €18 (all prices include one drink); metro: Cuitadella-Vila Olímpica;

map p.139 D1

A shrine to everything that sums up decadent nightlife. Predictable but popular music is blasted across the dance floor while the near-nude bar staff serve shots to eager punters. If you have the money to burn and hanker for a glorious combination of flash and trash, this is a one-stop dream come true.

#### CDLC
Passeig Marítim 32; tel: 93 224 0470; www.cdlcbarcelona.com; Mon–Wed 10pm–2.30am, Thur–Sun noon–3am; free; metro: Ciutedella-Vila Olímpica; map p.139 D1

See and be seen in this

**Left:** a flyer advertising fun and good times at Baja Beach.

Its weekly Bassline party (Fridays) offers a welcome departure from the city's passion for tech-house, with reggae, dancehall and drum 'n' bass until dawn.

### La Terrrazza
Poble Espanyol, Avda Marquès de Comillas; tel: 93 272 4980; www.laterrrazza.com; May–mid-Oct: Thur–Sat midnight–6am; admission charge €15–€18 (including first drink); metro: Espanya; map p.136 B4

Often seen as the jewel in the nightlife crown, the large outdoor dance floor sees an ocean of preened and pampered clubbers moving to the techno beats of DJ Sergio Patricio. The older sister to Fellini (see p.94), this club has been the victim of a bureaucratic crackdown on noise complaints – having been forced to close down for almost a year. Thankfully, it has re-emerged to consolidate its reputation.

## The Eixample

### Antilla Latin Club
C/Aragó 141; tel: 93 237 9324; www.antillasalsa.com; Tue–Sat 11.30pm–6am, Sun from 9pm; admission charge €10 (including one drink); metro: Urgell; map p.133 D1

A mainstay on the city's Latin club circuit, this *salsoteca* is the city's neon-lit answer to all your Cuban cravings. Live bands and DJs play bachata, merengue, and salsa till sunrise.

### Danzarama
Gran Via de les Corts Catalanes 604; tel: 93 301 9743, reservations: 93 342 5070; www.danzarama.com; Mon–Sat 7pm–3am; free; metro: Universitat; map p.134 A1

Downstairs from the somewhat swanky restaurant, it is possible to find an excellent starting point to any night.

### Suite Royale
Passeig Joan de Borbó 54; tel: 93 268 0012; nightly 10pm–4am; free; metro: Barceloneta; map p.138 B1

As a replacement to the recently closed Café Royale, this recently opened jazz-funk-infused lounge bar has become a popular destination for the late-night crowd. An intimate, retro-feel décor adds to the relaxed ambiance.

## Montjuïc, Poble Sec and Sant Antoni

### Apolo/Apolo 2
C/Nou de la Rambla 113; tel: 93 441 4004; www.sala-apolo.com; Wed–Sat 12.30–5am; admission charge €15 (including first drink); metro: Paral·lel; map p.137 D2

These neighbouring clubs/concert venues attract a similar crowd of smiley, seasoned club kids, though they radiate different vibes – Apolo is all chandeliers and soaring Deco glamour, while Apolo 2 is smaller and sleeker. The music in each runs the gamut from indie to electronica, depending on the night, and both clubs also host live bands.

### Maumau Underground
C/Fontrondona 33; tel: 93 441 8015; Thur 11pm–2.30am,

Fri–Sat 11pm–3am; one time 'membership fee' €5; metro: Paral·lel; map p.137 D2

Your first beer is free at this laid-back lounge club, housed in a converted warehouse in Poble Sec. DJs play a mix of funk, soul and hip hop, and special events (film screenings and exhibitions) are a regular feature. A good place to start before heading to the neighbouring Apolo clubs.

### Sala Instinto
C/Méxic 7, Plaça Espanya; tel: 93 424 8331; www.salainstinto.com; Wed–Sat midnight–6am, Sun 9pm–4am; admission charge €10 (including one drink); metro: Espanya or Hostafrancs; map p.136 B4

Party your socks (or shirt) off at this generally packed two-floor club by Plaça Espanya.

> **Transportation:** Metro hours are Sun–Thur 5am–midnight, and Fri 5am–2am; on Saturdays it runs all night, and is safe and packed until dawn. There's a good, if confusing, system of night buses (called Nitbús) that run every 20 minutes from Plaça Catalunya (you can check routes on www.tmb.net). Remember, too, that the old city is easily crossed on foot and that even Gràcia's just 20 minutes from Plaça Catalunya.

**Late-night eats:** Most restaurants close about 1am, but the city is rich with the big three of late-night dining: pizza, doughnuts, and doner kebabs. Some reliable choices: **Pizza del Borne** (Passeig del Borne 22, Born), excellent quality and price; **Top Döner** (Rambla de Raval 22; Raval), the best in Barcelona; the Barri Gòtic has snack joints aplenty on Calle Ferran. Try **Bocatta** (Pl. Sant Jaume) or **Maoz** (C/Ferran 13); Gràcia's **Churreria Joanic** (C/Escorial, Pl. Joanoc) is a post-club classic.

humping tunes, great ocktails, and a hip crowd nfuse anyone with the late night vibe.

**Sala BeCool**
Pl. Joan Llongueras 5; tel: 93 362 0413; www.salabecoll.com; ri–Sat 1pm–5.30am, Sun 10pm–5am; admission charge €8–€12 (Including one drink); metro: Hospital-Clinic, FGC: Muntaner; map p.133 D4
One of the city's premier dance clubs, its two rooms are divided by theme: the first s reserved for concerts and hen DJ sets (with minimal electro featuring strongly); he second for sounds-of-ow indie rock played by esident and guest DJs.

**Space Barcelona**
C/Tarragona 122; tel: 93 320 4200; www.spacebarcelona.com; ri–Sat midnight–6am, Sun 9pm–3am; admission charge €12–€15 (including first drink); metro: Tarragona; map p.132 C1
Cashing in on its more amous Balearic sister, Space attracts a younger crowd of igh-street-clad clubbers as well as some diehard club unnies to its dance floor. Deep House and even deeper ass adds to the minimalist écor which features four ars and virtually no seating.

## Upper Neighbourhoods

### Danzatoria
Avda Tibidabo 61, Tibidabo; tel: 93 211 6261; www.danzatoria-barcelona.com; Tue, Wed 11pm–2.30am, Thur–Sat 11pm–3am; free; FGC to Avda Tibidabo then 10 min walk
Beautiful people in a stunning uptown location. A converted mansion on a hill overlooking Barcelona plays host to an upmarket crowd wanting to dance the night away or simply lounge in one of the many spaces that are on offer. During the summer, the gardens are a spectacular bonus.

### Duvet
C/Córcega 327; tel: 93 237 4424; www.duvet.es; Sat 12.30–6am; admission charge €14; metro: Diagonal; map p.134 B3
New entry on the nightlife scene, Duvet attracts a high-end crowd to its glossy interior. A fabulous retro bar and funky house music ensures that this venue is always full to capacity.

### Heliogabal
Ramón y Cajal 80; www.heliogabal.com; nightly from 9.30pm; admission charge up to €5; metro: Joanic; map p.134 C4
Gràcia's artsy crowd congregates here to capacity in this low-key neighbourhood nightspot. Every

night is different, with live bands, cinema nights and art openings in constant rotation, with the focus usually on local talent.

### KGB
C/Alegre de Dalt 55; tel: 93 210 5906; www.salakgb.net; Fri–Sat 12.30–5.00am; admission charge €12 (including first drink); metro: Joanic or Alfons X
Club nights at this industrial-looking space in Gràcia attract a largely male crowd of hard-techno fans – but every now and then it hosts a stellar guest DJ and attracts friendlier and more variable partiers. It is advisable to check its schedule before heading up the hill. It's not advisable to turn up before 3am.

### Liquid
Avda de Manuel Azaña 21, L'Hospitalet; www.liquidbcn.com; summer: Sun midnight–5.30am; admission charge €15; metro: Zona Universitaria
Summertime clubbing classic, largely thanks to the is-this-really-a-good-idea swimming pool on the massive terrace. Hosts impressive names in electronic music on a weekly basis. Worth the trek, if you like your beats repetitive and your parties good and debauched.

# Pampering

In a city that has always taken itself a bit too seriously to bother with such frivolity, pampering is still a relatively new concept to *barcelonins*. The last couple of years, however, have seen a shift in temperament, with a number of day spa-type places springing up throughout the city, while hotels have been quick to add luxury spas to their list of facilities. It is now possible to squander a small fortune on your hands, feet and private parts as well as the more customary faces and bodies. But this being Barcelona, it is also possible to do it on the cheap. This chapter lists some choice spas, as well as a selection of places to stock up on beauty products.

## Cosmetics and Skincare

### Adonia
C/Aribau 138, Eixample; tel: 93 451 2350; Mon–Sat 10am–2.30pm, 4–8.30pm; metro: Diagonal or Hospital Clínic; map p.134 A3
This newly opened natural skincare store is a one-stop shop for ethically sound and environmentally conscious products such as Weleda, Caudalie and Dr Hauschka, with a 'green' spa to come.

### Florame
C/Enric Granados 37, Eixample; tel: 93 451 5556; www.florame.com.es; Mon–Sat 10am–8.30pm; metro: Universitat; map p.134 A2
Organic essential oils from the south of France form the core business of this smart little shop. Its range includes a good selection of some of the lesser-known oils such as basil and cinnamon, as well as a good skincare range for men and women.

### Paquita Ors
C/Padilla 254, Eixample; tel: 93 455 7032; www.cosmeticos-paquita-ors.com; Mon–Sat 10am–1.30pm, 5pm–8.15pm; metro: Sagrada Familia; map p.135 E3

**Call ahead:** In most cases you can't just walk in off the street and expect a massage or treatment at Barcelona's spas or treatment centres. Reservations are therefore essential.

Notoriously vain, and famous for living for years in a suite at the Ritz in Madrid, Paquita Ors is a true Spanish treasure. But do not expect to shop and go in this store. Your skin will be analysed, tested and prodded before they sell you anything, but you'll walk away with the finest, and prettiest, skincare routine you have ever had.

## Perfume

### La Galería de Santa María Novella
C/Espasería 4–8, Born; tel: 93 268 0237; Tue–Sat 10am–1.30pm, 5–8.30pm; metro: Jaume I; map p.138 C2
The stained-glass windows and intricately tiled floors make this perhaps the most beautiful perfumery in Spain. Saint María Novella was a nun in Florence who founded an apothecary, making flower, herb and spice remedies in

1612. This is its first Spanish outlet, and the handmade perfumes, oils and lotions are gifts you will treasure forever.

### Regia
Passeig de Gràcia 39, Eixample; tel: 93 216 0121; www.regia.es; Mon–Sat 10am–8.30pm; metro: Passeig de Gràcia; map p.134 B2
For those with the 'nose', the flagship store of the oldest perfume shop in town has a magical museum attached, filled with ancient bottles, potions and powder boxes dating back as far as the ancient Egyptians. Aside from which it stocks all the usual and latest brands.

## Spas

### Aqua Urban Spa
Gran de Gràcia 7, Gràcia; tel: 92 238 4160; www.aqua-urbanspa.com; Mon–Fri 9am–9.30pm, Sat 9.30am–8.30pm; metro: Fontana; map p.134 B3
This classy uptown venture focuses on good old-fashioned water treatments. Simply float from water jet massage, to jacuzzi, to steam room, to sauna, and if that is not enough, you can have a Dead Sea mud body

**Left and below:** A mà Teràpies.

wet room while admiring bedazzling views of the sea.

## Spaciomm

Hotel Omm, C/Rosselló 265, Eixample; tel: 93 445 4949; www.spaciomm.es; Mon–Sat 9am–10pm, Sun 10am–6pm: metro: Diagonal; map p.134 B3

A spa to see and be seen in, this swanky addition to the Hotel Omm (see p.70) has a wellness centre, water treatments and a make-over centre for a whole new you. Be sure to try the cava waterfalls, and top off your tan in sight of La Pedrera (see p.82).

## Therapy Centres

### A mà Teràpies

C/Enric Granados 23 2º2ª, Eixample; tel: 93 451 6572; www.amaterapies.org; Mon–Sat 10am–10pm, Sun noon–6pm by appointment; metro: Universitat; map p.134 A1

Soothing consultations in candle lit rooms make you feel better instantly at A mà. The extensive range of top-class treatments include a mind-boggling array of massage, deep cleansing facials, allergy testing and nutrition advice. It also boasts hands down the best pedicure in town. Specialists in treating mothers-to-be, this is a sure bet for getting your aches and pains sorted.

wrap as well. A water circuit pass costs €51.

## The Chi Spa

Club Turó David Lloyd, Avda Diagonal 673–685, Les Corts; tel: 93 447 2319; www.thechispa.com; Mon–Fri 10am–8pm, Sat 10am–6pm; metro: Zona Universitat

The place that's got *Vogue España* drooling. Sleek, Asian-style décor, and hip products have lured the Spanish a-list, who also come for the centre's star treatment: a Japanese anti-ageing concoction involving grapefruit, white clay and balsamic vinegar. Ironically, The Chi Spa also reads the *chispa* – meaning the gossip in English. And you can bet your bottom dollar that is what they do.

## Iradier

C/Escoles Pies 105, Bonanova; tel: 93 254 1717; www.iradier.com; Mon–Fri 7.45am–10pm, Sat and Sun 11am–7pm; FCG: Sarrià

This uptown women's-only wellness centre is one of the city's best-kept secrets. Set in a powder-pink villa and surrounded by grass lawns and turquoise pools with a decent health-food restaurant, it is well worth the small effort it takes to get there. Day passes cost €40.

## Six Senses at the Arts

C/Marina 19–21, Waterfront; tel: 93 224 7067; www.sixsenses.com; daily 9.30am–9pm; metro: Ciutadella-Vila Olímpica; map p.139 D2

If you have money to burn, this is the ultimate indulgence. This spa's location on the 43rd floor of the city's poshest hotel (see p.68) makes it the most spectacular in town. Book well in advance for one of its signature four-hand massages, and allow plenty of time to soak away your cares in the

# Parks, Gardens and Beaches

For many years the Parc de la Ciutadella was the city's only park, but over the last century land has steadily been donated for green space, and now parks and gardens dot every neighbourhood. The beaches, too, are a relatively recent addition to the *barcelonins'* leisure options, having been dredged up and scrubbed down in time for the 1992 Olympic Games. Nowadays it is difficult to believe the city lived with its 'back to the sea', as they say. All the parks listed here are free to enter unless otherwise stated.

## Beaches

Barcelona's beaches were only really created in the run-up to the Olympics, and are composed of tons of imported sand. This artificial aspect means that they are occasionally ravaged by storms then replaced at vast expense, but many would argue that they have paid for themselves several times over with the added tourist appeal. It's not only the tourists that are lured by the lapping of the waves, however; every morning, locals come down in their towelling dressing gowns to swim in all weathers, play dominoes, gossip and get fit. In summer the beaches get very crowded and noisy by midday, but then comes the lunchtime exodus.

### BARCELONETA TO THE FÒRUM

Roughly speaking, the further north you walk, the quieter the beaches. Liveliest are those south of the Port Olímpic: Platja Barceloneta and Platja Passeig Marítim. For more, and cleaner, sand, however, head to the stretch beginning with the Platja Nova Icària, which then becomes Bogatell, Mar Bella, Nova Mar Bella and finally Llevant, reclaiming a seafront that had been cut off by railway lines, yards and warehouses. This last is popular with families and women relaxing alone and is an easy walk from the metro El Maresme–Fòrum.

## Sant Pere and Born

### Parc de la Ciutadella
Passeig de Pujades/Passeig de Picasso; daily 10am–sunset; metro: Arc de Triomf/Barceloneta; map p.139 C2–D3
The park's name has its origins in the citadel that Felipe V had constructed on this land after the fall of Barcelona in 1714, demolishing 40 streets and making thousands homeless. In 1869 the land was ceded to the city, but it was not until 1888, the year of the World Exposition, that the park began to be a reality.

Interesting buildings remain from its military past and from

**Left:** a Barcelona beach.
**Right:** Parc de la Ciutadella.

**Left:** Gaudí's mosaic benches in the Park Güell.

Information on any of the parks listed here can be found by calling 010 from inside Barcelona.

designed by French landscape architect J.C.N. Forestier. The statue in the lake is *El Desconsol*, one of Catalan sculptor Josep Llimona's most highly regarded pieces.
SEE ALSO CHILDREN, P.37; MUSEUMS AND GALLERIES, P.86

### The Waterfront and Poblenou

#### Cementiri de Poblenou
C/Taulat 2, Poblenou; tel: 93 484 1999/93 225 1661; www. cbsa.es; daily 8am–6pm; free; metro: Llacuna
The first cemetery in the city, built in 1775 and originally situated outside the city walls, this is a fascinating and pleasant spot for a walk. Many of those buried here were victims of the yellow fever that swept Barcelona in 1821, and a monument in the centre commemorates their deaths. As well as the grand family pantheons, the cemetery is notable for its impressive sculptures, most famously the sinister *Kiss of*

Note that while the official timetable for municipal parks is 10am to sunset, in practice most open up to two hours earlier with the arrival of the gardeners, and close later, particularly in summer when they form crucial venues for outdoor concerts and festivals.

its glorious time as the Exposition showground, but the most remarkable aspect of the park is its refreshing tranquillity. It is a real park, full of skateboards and footballs, prams and toddlers. There are pedalos for hire, as well as rowing boats on the lake. Constantly tended by municipal gardeners, the park is verdant, scented and shady, a soothing place to walk in all seasons.

Points of interest include the Cascada, the monumental fountain and artificial lake in the northern corner; the **Zoo**; the Modernista Castell dels Tres Dragons, now housing the **Zoological Museum** (part of the park's Museu de la Ciències Naturals); and the Plaça d'Armes, where there is a serene, oval formal garden

**Left:** the Cementiri
de Poblenou.

ern marshland and wacky
planted areas that still need
to reach maturation, it is a
great alternative for a picnic.

### Montjuïc, Poble Sec and Sant Antoni

#### Jardí Botànic
C/Doctor Font i Quer; tel: 93 426
4935; daily 10am–sunset;
admission charge; metro:
Espanya, or Funicular de
Montjuïc; map p.136 B2
Spread over 15 hectares
(37½ acres), Montjuïc's
botanic garden has sustain-
ability as its buzzword, and
contains only plants from five
areas sharing near-identical
climates; the Mediterranean
basin, California, Chile,
Australia and South Africa.
Many of these are in their
infancy, as the garden is only
a few years old, but there is
still much of interest, and the
views are unbeatable.

#### Jardins Costa i Llobera
Carretera de Miramar 1; daily
10am–sunset; Funicular de
Montjuïc or bus: 50; map p.137
D1
Once a strategic defence
point for the city, the Buena-
vista battery, this is now a
cactus garden, described by
the *New York Times* as one of
the best gardens in the
world, though the roar of
traffic below can be off-
putting. It has cacti from
Mexico, Bolivia, Africa and
California.

#### Jardins Laribal
Passeig de Santa Madrona;
daily 10am–sunset; metro:
Poble Sec; map p.136 C3
Designed by J.C.N Forestier
between 1916 and 1922,
these shady gardens tumble
down from the **Fundació**

*Death*. There are 30-minute
guided tours in Spanish and
Catalan on the first and third
Sundays of the month.

#### Parc de Diagonal Mar
Avda Diagonal y Cinturón Ronda
Litoral; metro: Selva de Mar
Bizarre it may be – think 21st-
century Alice in Wonderland –
but local architects Enric
Miralles (died 2000) and
Benedetta Tagliabue have
excelled in coming up with
something different this time.
With its peephole walls and
mad network of paths leading
to even crazier sculptures,
kiddies' games areas, a mod-

**Left:** the surrealist Parc de
Diagonal Mar.

Joan Miró and the **Teatre Grec**, and are a pleasant way to descend from Montjuïc. The stone steps flanked by running water are based on those of the Alhambra palace in Granada, and tucked away in one corner is a pretty, formal rose garden.

## The Eixample

### Jardins de la Torre de les Aigües
C/Roger de Llúria 56; tel: 93 423 4350; 25 June–2 Sept: Mon–Sat 10am–8pm, Sun 10am–3pm; admission charge; metro: Girona; map p.134 B2
Tucked inside one of the Eixample blocks is this small garden with a wonderful 'beach' for young children, with sand and a shallow pool. There are showers, toilets and a bar.

### Parc de l'Estació del Nord
C/Almogàvers; daily 10am–sunset; metro: Arc de Triomf/Marina; map p.139 D4
A small grassy park adjacent to the main city bus station and notable for the soaring azure 'land sculptures' by Beverley Pepper.

### Parc Joan Miró
C/Tarragona; daily 10am–sunset; metro: Espanya/Tarragona; map p.133 C1
Covering four Eixample blocks, the arid Parc Joan Miró is also known as the Parc de l'Escorxador because it was the location of the municipal slaughterhouse until 1979. It is worth a visit for the 22-metre (70ft) Miró statue *Dona i Ocell* (Woman and Bird), striking in its simple setting on a small island in the middle of a pool in the park. One of Miró's last works, it was unveiled in 1983, just a few months before he died.

## Upper Neighbourhoods

### Parc del Castell de l'Oreneta
C/Montevideo 45, Sarrià; daily

The life-size mammoth behind the boating lake in Parc de la Ciutadella *(see p.100)* was supposed to be joined by 11 similarly huge dinosaurs as part of an educational project at the beginning of the last century. Sadly Norbert Font i Sagué, whose idea it was, died before it could come to fruition, but the mammoth is still one of the park's most loved features.

10am–sunset; FGC: Reina Elisenda
The Oreneta forms a link between the city and the range of Collserola hills beyond, affording great views from its pine-scented walks. A particular favourite with the kids, it has a miniature train that runs on Sundays and pony rides at weekends. There is also a basic restaurant serving spit-roast chicken.

### Parc de Cervantes
Avda Diagonal 706, Pedralbes; daily 10am–sunset; metro: Zona Universitaria
A pocket of green in an otherwise uninspiring part of town, the Parc de Cervantes is useful for a picnic stop after a visit to the Pedralbes monastery (there are few restaurants in the area). It has especially good installations for children, a striking sculpture by Andreu Alfaro and an extensive rose garden, best enjoyed in late spring.

### Park Güell
C/Olot; tel: 93 285 6899; May–Sept: daily 10am–9pm, Apr and Oct: 10am–8pm, Mar and Nov: 10am–7pm, Dec–Feb: 10am–6pm; free; metro: Vallcarca
Gaudí's fantastical Park Güell wants for grassy spaces but is unbeatable for its

Modernista features, particularly the vast terrace surrounded by one long, colourfully tiled bench, with views all the way out to sea.
SEE ALSO MODERNISME, P.83

### Parc del Laberint
C/Germans Desvalls/Passeig Castanyers, Horta; daily 10am–sunset; admission charge; metro: Mundet
An extensive, leafy park, with formal gardens and many shady walkways. Its main attraction, however, is the fiendish maze that gives it its name. Bringing food inside is not permitted, but there is a picnic zone outside the entrance.

### Turó Parc
Avda Pau Casals, Sant Gervasi; daily 10am–sunset; FGC: Muntaner; map p.133 D4
Also known as Jardins Poeta Marquina, the Turó Parc was a project of landscape architect Rubió i Tudurí, and has two distinct areas. One is made up of lawn, hedges and flower beds laid out in a classic geometric pattern, the other contains children's playgrounds, a small lake and an open-air theatre. Sculptures by Clarà and Viladomat, among others, dot the interior of the park.

**Right:** Park Güell's much-photographed mosaic lizard.

# Restaurants

**B**arcelona's restaurant scene is lively, varied and, above all, great value for money. Providing you avoid total tourist traps (it's impossible to avoid tourists altogether in Barcelona), standards are high and getting higher thanks to the city's reputation as Europe's dining hot spot. Celebrity chefs have set a precedent for quality, imaginative cooking, and it is now possible to eat somewhere different every night without breaking the bank, as up-and-coming cooks go all out to win the hearts of their dining public. *See also Bars and Cafés, p.28–35; Food and Drink, p.54–7; Tapas Bars, p.120–3*

## Barri Gòtic

CATALAN
**Agut**
C/Gignàs 16; tel: 93 315 1709;
Tues–Sat 1.30–4pm,
9–11.45pm, Sun 1.30–4pm; €€;
metro: Jaume I; map p.138 B2
This bustling, noisy, traditional restaurant has heaps of atmosphere and walls plastered with oils. Good for rubbing shoulders with well-heeled *barcelonins* and for deeply satisfying Catalan specialities such as beef stews and *fetge* with spinach.
**Cafè de l'Acadèmia**
C/Lledó 1; tel: 93 315 0026;
Mon–Fri 9am–noon, 1.30–5pm,
8.45pm–1am; €€; metro:
Jaume I; map p.138 B3
An Old Quarter classic serving new twists on old favourites such as roast game birds and creamy rice dishes. The intimate candlelit dining room buzzes with chatter over

Prices for an average three-course meal with wine:
€ under €25
€€ €25–€40
€€€ €40–€60
€€€€ over €60

Avoid eating on Plaça de Catalunya and La Rambla as restaurants on the whole tend to be overpriced and poor quality.

lunch midweek, while tables on the medieval Plaça Sant Just make it one of the loveliest summer dining destinations. Booking essential.
**Can Culleretes**
C/Quintana 5; tel: 93 317 3022;
Tue–Sat 1.30–4pm, 9–11pm,
Sun 1.30–4pm; €; metro: Liceu;
map p.138 B3
The oldest continuously functioning restaurant in town dates back to 1786 and is as popular now as ever. The rabbit warren of dining rooms heaves with tourists and locals alike come to enjoy rib-sticking traditional fare of pork and prunes, goose and pears and beefy stews with mushrooms. Booking essential.
**Nonell**
Plaça Isidre Nonell s/n 3; tel: 93 301 1378; www.nonell.es; Mon–Sun 1–4pm, 8pm–midnight; €€; metro: Jaume I; map p.138 B3
Just a minute away from the tour groups congregating in the cathedral square, you will

find this stylish restaurant on a hidden plaça. Acacia trees shade the terrace tables, while a cheerful tangerine interior makes a lively backdrop to updated Catalan classics like *mar y muntanya*, a rich concoction of squid and blood sausage finished with a fluffy pea foam.
**Taxidermista**
Plaça Reial 8; tel: 93 412 4536;
Tue–Sun 1pm–1am; €; metro:
Liceu; map p.138 B3
No prizes for guessing the not-too-distant origins of this elegant addition to the otherwise very average line-up of restaurants in Plaça Reial. Stylishly renovated from its former role into an airy, luminous space where innovative Catalan dishes like octopus terrine and poached farm eggs with smoked Idiazábal cheese are served.

JAPANESE
**Shunka**
C/Sagristans 5; tel: 93 412 4991; Mon–Fri 1.30–3.30pm, Sat–Sun 2–4pm, 8.30–11.30pm; €€€; metro: Jaume I; map p.138 B3
If the celebrity chefs are going

**Left:** carnivore heaven at Vino Tinto Parrilla, *see p.111.*

1535; www.matsuri-restaurante. com; Mon–Thur 1.30–3.30pm, 8.30–11.30pm, Fri 1.30–3.30pm, 8.30pm–midnight, Sat 8.30pm–midnight; €; metro: Jaume I; map p.138 B3
A slice of Southeast Asia tucked away in the Old Quarter, with teak wood furniture and tinkling water features. Bright-tasting dishes are laden with fresh aromatic herbs and salt, sour and spicy layers.

### Sant Pere and Born

CATALAN
**Orígens 99.9%**
C/Vidrieria 6–8; tel: 93 310 7531; daily 12.30am–1.30am; €; metro: Jaume I; map p.138 C2
Handily located right in the heart of the Born's shopping quarter, Orígens combines a restaurant and deli that sticks strictly to Catalan food and wine. Menus that you can take away are loaded with recipes to recreate at home. Of several franchises dotted around town, this wood-panelled dining room is the prettiest and the best.
**Pla de la Garsa**
C/Assaonadors 13; tel: 93 315 2413; Mon–Sun 8pm–midnight; €€; metro: Jaume I; map p.138 C3

out to play they often kick off the evening here, where they're treated to a dazzling array of some of the city's finest sushi. Mere mortals can ask for the same treatment or choose from a menu that incorporates everything from udon to luscious toro sashimi. Key here is to sit at the bar – it's just not the same at a table – and be prepared to experiment. Also a good option if you're dining solo.

MEDITERRANEAN
**El Gran Café**
C/Avinyó 9; tel: 93 318 7986; Sun–Thur 1–4.30pm, 5.30pm–midnight, Fri–Sat 1–4.30pm, 5.30pm–12.30am; €€; metro: Jaume I; map p.138 B3
A splendid bistro-style eatery with Parisian overtones: polished wood, tiled floors, white linen tables cloths and formal waiting staff. They do a good-value set lunch, offering a mix of Parisian staples like French onion soup and duck confit, with Catalan classics like *escalivada* and *fideuá*. Handy if you want to eat early or late.

PERUVIAN
**Peimong**
C/Templers 6; tel: 93 318 2873; Tue–Sat 1–4pm, 8–11.30pm, Sun 1–4pm; €; metro: Jaume I; map p.138 B3
A small, simple restaurant serving authentic *ceviche* (raw fish marinated in lime juice with coriander and hot chilli peppers) and other Peruvian specialities – though no guinea pig – washed down with Peruvian beers and Inca Kola.

SOUTHEAST ASIAN
**Matsuri**
Plaça Regomir 1; tel: 93 268

**Right:** Orígens 99.9%.

This tastefully restored medieval stable with colourful tiles and bow-beamed ceilings is a peaceful option for *pica-pica*. Do as locals do and order a platter of cheeses, pâtés and *embotits* (cured sausages, ham and typical pork products) washed down with fruity rosado wine from the Penedès. A good-value tasting menu is also available if you are unsure what to order.

**Senyor Parellada**
C/Argentería 37; tel: 93 310 5094; daily 1–4pm, 8.30pm–midnight; €€; metro: Jaume I; map p.138 B3

Prices for an average three-course meal with wine:
€ under €25
€€ €25–€40
€€€ €40–€60
€€€€ over €60

One of very few restaurants in town focused on serving traditional Catalan dishes such as *esqueixada* (salt cod with onions, olive and tomatoes), roast leg of lamb with 12 heads of garlic and hearty *botifarra amb mongetes* (sausage and beans). Half-portions are available, which adds more scope for the gluttony, and the delightful dining room set around a cobalt-blue dining room with huge chandeliers makes eating here a special occasion.

**Set Portes**
Passeig Isabel II 14; tel: 93 319 3033; www.7portes.com; Mon–Sun 1pm–1am; €€€; metro: Barceloneta; map p.138 C2
Over 160 years old and still going strong, this sympathetically restored restaurant has served a number of bigwigs through the years, among them Winston Churchill and

Che Guevara. While the food isn't quite always as it should be, there is no faulting the atmosphere in the bustling dining room, and it is especially popular for family Sunday lunches. There's a rice dish for every day of the week, as well as a good-value set lunch.

### DESSERTS
**Espai Sucre**
C/Princesa 53; tel: 93 268 1630; www.espaisucre.com; Tue–Sat 9–11.30pm; €€€; metro: Jaume I; map p.139 C3
'Dinner' is not quite the word at Jordi Butrón's revolutionary restaurant that serves mainly *postres* (there is the odd token savoury dish). We're not talking apple crumble here, but creations that play with the palate, like lychee soup with celery, apples and eucalyptus and lapsang

*Left:* Senyor Parellada.

souchong-infused ice cream. An excellent range of dessert wines accompany the three- or five-course pudding menu.

## PAN ASIAN
### Mosquito
C/Carders 46 baixos 2a; tel: 93 268 7569; www.mosquitotapas. com; Tue–Sun 1pm–1am; €; metro: Arc de Triomf or Jaume I; map p.138 C3

'Exotic tapas' is a modest assessment of the small Asian dishes served at this convivial and lively neighbourhood bar. Good form is to order several dishes – as you would tradi- tional tapas – and share them: delicious potato chaat, bacalao tom yam, and aubergine gyoza. Even better is the newly opened sushi bar that does superb sashimi and wonderful silken tofu topped with soy and fluttering bonito flakes. The wine list is carefully chosen, along with a handful of German brews.

### Wushu
C/Marquès de l'Argentera 1; tel: 93 310 7313; www.wushu- restaurant.com; Mon–Sun 1pm–midnight; €; metro: Barceloneta; map p.138 C2

Recently moved to a new location with navy paintwork and subtle Japanese cartoons, the ever-popular Wushu continues to thrill and delight a sea of fans. Brad's top-notch Southeast Asian cooking includes a couple of daily specials such as tuna in sour curry, with a solid reper- toire of regular favourites including a rich and hearty king prawn laksa, a Thai duck red curry, a thoroughly addic- tive green papaya salad with seductive heat and a to-die- for dessert list (particularly the steamed ginger pudding).

*Right:* Asian tapas at Mosquito.

**Street food:** Sometimes there's so much to cram into a short weekend that a sit-down meal seems a terrible waste. The following are great for eating on the run. For picnics on the beach in Barceloneta try the fresh stuffed *piadinas* (Italian flat-bread sandwiches) at C/Meer 48, DIY noodles hot from the wok at Wokimarket at Passeig Marítim 1, and jumbo sandwiches named after city streets at SDWCH on C/Pesca- teria 6. In the Barri Gòtic Frank- furt Sant Jaume on Plaça Sant Jaume is great for a hotdog; you can get cava-battered fish and chips on the Rambla del Raval, and lively Japanese at Sushi Express on C/Consell de Cent 255.

## Raval
### CATALAN
### Elisabets
C/Elisabets 2; tel: 93 317 5826; Mon–Sat 7am–11pm; €; metro: Catalunya; map p.138 A4

A typically down-at-heel Raval institution, this bar- cum-cafeteria is bright, smoky, noisy and crowded, with folk shoehorning them- selves in like starving sardines. The tapas and *combinados* (mixed plates) are excellent hangover fodder leaning towards the heavier end of the spectrum. Try their hearty osso bucco or chickpea stews, and heavy duty *bocadillos*. The lunch menu is also good value.

### Mam i Teca
C/Lluna 4; tel: 93 441 3335; Wed–Mon, Sun 1–4pm, 8.45–midnight, Sat 8.45– midnight; €; metro: Liceu/Sant Antoni; map p.138 A4

Mama i Teca is easy to miss, but don't. Convivial hosts Robin and Alfons entertain with ongoing banter and mis- chief, while serving superlative home-made Catalan food. Daily dishes are chalked up on a blackboard and depend largely on Alfons's whim: if the beef stew with *rovellons* (wild mushrooms) makes an appearance, order it. Other- wise there's a good range for tapas to take the edge off your hunger, followed by

107

heaping platters of perfectly cooked lamb chops, boat-fresh grilled sole, and one of the juiciest filet steaks you will ever eat. This intimate space with yellow walls and well-stocked bar has only six tables, so book in advance to be sure of a seat.

## MEDITERRANEAN
### Ànima

C/Àngels 6; tel: 93 342 4912; Mon–Thur 1–4pm, 9pm–12.30am, Fri–Sat 1–4pm, 9pm–1.15am; €€; metro: Catalunya; map p.138 A4

A leafy pavement terrace near the MACBA (see p.87–8) with a designer interior makes a good setting for the delicious dishes presented like artworks by this young chef. His travels have clearly set a precedent in his direction, offering playful dishes such as melon soup with crayfish and monkfish in a pistachio crust. The lunchtime menu is exceptional value.

### Bar Lobo

C/Pintor Fortuny 3; tel: 93 481 5346; www.grupotragaluz.com/barlobo; Mon–Wed, Sun noon–midnight, Thur–Sat noon–2am; €; metro: Catalunya; map p.138 A4

The youngest, hippest member of the Tragaluz empire attracts a party-going crowd with its slick, minimalist interior, terrace on a busy pedestrian street, and light Mediterranean dishes. Open late for drinks at weekends.

### Bar Ra

Plaça de la Gardunya 3; tel: 93 301 4163; Mon–Sat 9.45am–12.30am; €; metro: Liceu; map p.138 A3

Even in the winter this large, colourful terrace behind the Boqueria market is a taste of the Caribbean and a major suntrap, so be prepared to queue or get here early. Food is good value, though it can

---

**Dining with the stars:** The list of places with Michelin stars in Barcelona grows and grows, but you don't necessarily have to be rich to eat in them. In keeping with the tradition of offering workers a hearty lunchtime meal, some – not all – offer upmarket versions of the *menú del día* and the occasional tasting menu at prices that won't make you balk. **Alkimia**'s (C/Indústria 79; tel: 93 207 6115; map p.135 D3) five-course tasting menu costs €54; an eight-course menu at **Saüc** (Ptge Lluís Pellicer 12; tel: 93 321 0189; map p.133 E3) including cheeses costs €48; **Hofmann**'s (C/Granada del Penedès 14–16; tel: 93 218 7165) new uptown dining room does a lunchtime *menú del día* which changes daily and costs €39 for four courses; and the two-starred **ABAC** (Avda Tibidabo 1; tel: 93 319 6601), also with a new uptown restaurant, does an executive menu of three courses for €45.

---

occasionally slip a little in standards. When it is good it's very good, offering hearty salads, good baked fish and Mauritian chicken.

### Dos Trece

C/Carme 40; tel: 93 301 7306; www.dostrece.net; daily 10am–midnight; €; metro: Liceu; map p.138 A4

This lively and happening bar has a laid-back vibe, making it equally popular among the city's fashionable crowd as well as a clique of yummy mummies and pappies who take over the place for Sunday brunch and bloody Marys. Don't let that put you off: the burgers are great and the Moroccan lounge downstairs is a groovy place to digest.

**Right:** Kaiku serves excellent variations on classic dishes.

---

### Organic

C/Junta de Comerç 11; tel: 93 301 0902; www.organic.es; daily 12.30pm–midnight; €; metro: Liceu; map p.138 A3

One of the latest new-wave vegetarian restaurants, this one does it in style, with minimalist décor against a smart interior. Tables are communal, with a good choice of wholesome organic food such as hot spinach pie with melted cheese, and desserts. There is often live music at weekends, and there's a take-away branch in La Boqueria market (see p.78).

## The Waterfront and Poblenou

### ITALIAN
### Bestial

C/Ramón Trias i Fargas 2–4; tel: 93 224 0407; daily 8pm–1.30am; €€; metro: Vila Olímpica; map p.139 D1

What it lacks in wow factor when it comes to the food it makes up for by having the loveliest beach terrace in town. The multi-levelled wood-decked space is lushly planted with the odd lounging area and a cocktail bar. Peopled by beautiful

creatures (including the staff), this is a place to see and be seen in. Portions are small, but the risottos, pasta dishes and carpaccios are all decent enough. Perfect spot for after-dinner drinks Thur–Sat until 2am.

## MEDITERRANEAN
### Agua
Passeig Marítim 30; tel: 93 225 1272; www.grupotragaluz.com/agua; Mon–Thur 1.30–3.45pm, 8.30–11.30pm, Fri–Sat 1–4.30pm, 8pm–12.30am, Sun 1–4.30pm, 8–11.30pm; €€; metro: Vila Olímpica; map p.139 D1

This stylish, relaxed restaurant serves modern Mediterranean food, good fish dishes and satisfying paellas. The terrace is another gem, well protected from any breeze even in the winter months, perfect for tucking into a long lazy lunch. Booking essential.

### La Cova Fumada
C/Baluart 56; tel: 93 221 4061; Mon–Fri 9am–3.30pm, Thur–Fri 6–8.30pm, Sat 9am–1.30pm; €; metro: Barceloneta; map p.138 C1

Crammed, chaotic and charmingly down-at-heel, this is a true *bar de barrio* with napkins and toothpicks littering the floor and thick with local atmosphere. Grilled sardines and spicy *bombetas* (potato balls stuffed with meat and topped with chilli sauce and alioli) are must-haves. Note the slightly peculiar opening hours.

### Kaiku
Plaça del Mar 1; tel: 93 221 9082; Tue–Sun 1am–4pm; €€; metro: Barceloneta; map p.138 C2

A beachside favourite with aqua-green awnings and bustling atmosphere, Kaiku is not your typical paella joint. The chef sets high standards in a port beleaguered by overfishing by using sustainable fish and seafood with date of catch and source clearly marked. He also makes inventive salads such as shaved *fetge* with beetroot, and cooks a mean, if unconventional paella, using locally smoked rice as a base.

### El Lobito
C/Ginebra 9; tel: 93 319 9164; Tue–Sat noon–2am; €€€€; metro: Barceloneta; map p.138 C2

Prices for an average three-course meal with wine:
€ under €25
€€ €25–€40
€€€ €40–€60
€€€€ over €60

With possibly the best fish and seafood you will ever eat, this tiny wood-panelled dining room with an equally petit pavement terrace oozes atmosphere. There's no menu, and whatever is served will depend on what came into market that day, but you can expect magic. A tasting menu costs €75. Steep but sublime. Booking essential.

### La Oca Mar
Espigó Bac de Roda, Platja Mar Bella; tel: 93 225 0100; Mon–Sun 1pm–1am; €€; metro: Poblenou/Selva de Mar; map p.138 B2

Like a little island unto itself, at La Oca Mar you can wine and dine virtually in the sea. This spectacular restaurant, jutting out to sea on the breakwater, serves a good range of well-prepared seafood and local seasonal dishes. The *arroz negro* (rice

cooked in squid ink) and *arroz de bogavante* (lobster rice) are superlative. Lunchtime and weekend menus (around €10 and €16 respectively) are a bargain.

**El Suquet de l'Almirall**
Passeig Joan de Borbó 65; tel: 93 221 6233; Tue–Sat 1–4pm, 8.30–11pm; Sun 1–3.30pm; €€€; metro: Barceloneta; map p.138 B1
This comfortable, tastefully decorated restaurant with a small terrace overlooking the Port Vell is in a different league to its numerous neigh-

bours. Chef Quim Marqués has given new life to traditional Mediterranean favourites such as rice dishes and *suquet* (fish stew), with excellent results. The *menú ciego* (blind), which includes six tapas and a rice or fish dish, is good value at less than €40.

## Montjuïc, Poble Sec and Sant Antoni

### ARGENTINIAN
**El Laurel**
C/Floridablanca 140; tel: 93 325 6292; Mon–Sun 8pm–midnight; €; metro: Urgell or Sant Antoni; map p.137 D4
A top spot to have up your sleeve if you are heading to the Floridablanca cinema *(see p.53)* across the road. Laurel serves imaginative Argentinian *empanadas*, ranging from

standard meat and tuna, to cheese and celery, to squid in ink. The narrow bar is perpetually crowded, but there is a more spacious dining room at the rear serving tasty pizza.

### CATALAN
**Bodega Sepúlveda**
C/Sepúlveda 173 bis; tel: 93 323 5944; Mon–Fri 10am–12.30am, Sat 7.30pm–12.30am; €; metro: Urgell; map p.137 E4
A small family-run restaurant serving excellent home-made dishes. Much of it is stew-based, such as chickpeas with blood sausage, *callos* (tripe) and hearty stuffed squid, but there is also a good selection of less rib-sticking fare such as the house special: spicy, marinated tuna, baked artichokes and richly flavoured *escali-*

Prices for an average three-course meal with wine:
€ under €25
€€ €25–€40
€€€ €40–€60
€€€€ over €60

**Left:** the stylish dining area at Vino Tinto Parrilla.

vada (pepper and aubergine salad) topped with anchovies.

### Can Margarit
C/Concòrdia 21; tel: 93 441 6723; Mon–Sat 8.30–11.30pm; €; metro: Poble Sec; map p.137 C3

Great for atmosphere as much as anything else, this barn of a place lets you help yourself to wine from the barrel on arriving, and serves hearty country cooking to the masses. Particularly good here is the pan amb tomàquet, which you do yourself, otherwise it is herby rabbit stew, lamb chops and monster pork sausages thrown on a grill.

### ITALIAN
### La Bella Napoli
C/Margarit 12; tel: 93 442 5056; Mon 8.30pm–midnight, Tue 1.30–4pm, 8.30pm–midnight; €; metro: Paral·lel; map p.137 D3

Run by gregarious Neapolitans in 'Godfather' style apparel, this remains the city's best pizza joint. Light and crispy pies come with a myriad of toppings accompanied by Italian wines.

### MEDITERRANEAN
### Tapioles 53
C/Tapioles 53; tel: 93 329 2238; www.tapioles53.com; Tue–Sat 9–11.30pm; €€€; metro: Poble Sec or Paral·lel; map p.137 D3

Located in an old umbrella-making factory, this secret dining room in Poble Sec provides a home-style experience for clued-in foodies. Aussie chef Sarah Stothart offers a small, international menu inspired by top-quality ingredients sourced from all over Europe, like feta cheese from a remote Greek island, fresh pasta stuffed with pears and gorgonzola,

and wild mushrooms from woodland in the nearby wine country. Reservations essential.

### MOROCCAN
### Kasbah
C/Vila i Vila 82; tel: 93 329 8384; Tue–Sat 1–4pm, 8pm–midnight; €; metro: Paral·lel; map p.137 D2

Textiles, cushions and low tables create the right atmosphere for delicious Arabic food, predominantly Moroccan (couscous, tajine), but also Syrian and Lebanese specialities. Good for a romantic supper.

### THAI
### Thai Thai
C/Diputació 93; tel: 620 938 059; www.thaithai.es; daily 1–4pm, 8pm–midnight; €€; metro: Urgell; map p.133 D1

Authentic Thai cooking in a spacious and pleasant restaurant of red brick, bow-beams and fresh flowers on the table. Ideally it is somewhere to go with a larger

group, as the extensive menu makes it good for sharing. Dishes such as duck massaman curry, seafood with fresh coconut, satay and pad Thai noodles top the bill.

### The Eixample
### CASTILIAN
### Vino Tinto Parrilla
C/Aribau 27; tel: 93 451 1027; www.vintotinto.com; Mon–Sat 1–4pm, 8.45pm–midnight; €€; metro: Universitat; map p.134 A1

Warm up with a drink at the bar before moving through to this swish navy and timber warehouse-style dining room. Juicy t-bones, botifarra and chorizo sprinkled liberally with sea salt and seared over open flame washed down with powerful red wines are the order of the day here. Vegetarians need not apply.

### CATALAN
### Àpat
C/Aribau 137; tel: 93 439 6414; Tue–Sat 1–4pm, 8.30pm–midnight, Sun 1–4pm; €€; FGC: Provença; map p.134 A3

Contemporary Catalan cooking in a sleek, black-accented interior reminiscent of posh places in the 1980s. Still Oriol Vicente is a young chef showing lots of promise, with signature dishes such as fresh fig salad with sardines and octopus, and 'dirty' rice with cuttlefish and pork ribs. The lunch menu is exceptional value at €13.50 for three courses including wine.

### Casa Calvet
C/de Casp 48; tel: 93 412 4012; www.casacalvet.com; Mon–Sat 1–3.30pm, 8.30–11pm; €€€€; metro: Urquinaona; map p.134 C1

Satisfy gourmet and culture-vulture needs in one fell swoop at this top-class restaurant, housed in former textile offices designed by Gaudí. Intimate, cubicle-

Prices for an average three-course meal with wine:
€ under €25
€€ €25–€40
€€€ €40–€60
€€€€ over €60

style dining tables make it one of the best romantic restaurants in the city, with an equally seductive, regularly changing menu.

### Cinc Sentits

C/Aribau 58; tel: 93 323 9490; www.cincsentits.com; Mon 1.30–3.30pm, Tue–Sat 1.30–3.30pm, 8.30–11.15pm; €€€€; metro: Passeig de Gràcia or Universitat; map p.134 A2

Probably the best restaurant in town for modern Catalan cuisine; ingredients take on magical qualities in the hands of chef Jordi Artal. The sleek, minimal dining room provides a soothing backdrop to one inspired course after another, such as silky diver scallops nestling in a purée of Jerusalem artichokes, wild sea bass with foaming alioli and a divine suckling pig with Prior-

at wine and honey reduction. If you want to go all out, treat yourself to Jordi's omakase menu (in which he chooses for you), an eight-course extravaganza designed to surprise and delight.

### Gurqui

C/Mallorca 303, tel: 93 458 5216; Mon–Sat 7pm–2.30am; €€€€; metro: Diagonal; map p.134 C2

A clandestine restaurant in a basement location, this homey eatery with its second-hand mismatched furniture and flickering candlelight is a real find, if an expensive one. Serving top-notch, expensive yet simple ingredients like clams cooked in wine, and juicy tender steaks as well as locally sourced tapas, it is perfect for impressing a new-found lover with posh late-night eats.

### MEDITERRANEAN
### Fast Good

C/Balmes 127; tel: 93 452 2374; www.fast-good.com; €; daily noon–midnight; metro: Diagonal; map p.134 A3

Chef Ferran Adrìa is often

*Right:* the pop art-inspired Flash-Flash.

lauded as the best in the world, and if you can't afford to go to his restaurant El Bulli or wait a couple of years to get in, then you can at least treat yourself to a juicy gourmet burger at his flashy new fast food joint. Funky décor and hip waiting staff mean it is worth sticking around to eat in.

### La Verema

C/Comte d'Urgell 88; tel: 93 451 6891; Mon 1.30–4pm, Tue–Sat 1.30–4pm, 9–11pm; €€€; metro: Urgell; map p.133 E1

A little off the beaten track, but worth travelling for, this neat little local bistro offers great-value set lunches such as steak Paris and chicken curry, as well as the house special: oysters at the bar. It is also good for tapas focused on seasonal specials such as artichokes and wild mushrooms.

### TEX-MEX
### Mex & Cal

C/Aribau 50; tel: 93 323 4316; Mon–Thur 8pm–midnight, Fri–Sat 8pm–2am; €€; metro: Universitat; map p.134 A2

The best place to eat à la Baja California. Authentic and tasty nachos, burritos, plus cocktails in an attractive, animated atmosphere.

## Upper Neighbourhoods

### CASTILIAN
### Asador de Aranda

Avda del Tibidabo 31; tel: 93 417 0115; www.asadordearanda. com; €€€; metro: Tibidabo

If you don't mind the thought of eating a teeny tiny piglet, this is the best place in Barcelona to try old Castile's national dish of *cochinillo*.

*Left:* Fast Good, the hippest fast-food joint in town.

Here, in this totally OTT mansion with ornate dining rooms, the milk-fed critter comes whole in a terracotta casserole, running with juices, meltingly tender flesh and taut, crisp skin.

### Flash-Flash

C/Granada del Penedès 25; tel: 93 237 0990; €; Mon–Sun 1pm–1.30am; FCG: Gràcia; map p.134 A4

Almost a period piece now, this bar was super-trendy in the 1970s. Its wonderful white leatherette seating and black-and-white Warhol-type prints on the walls still have style, and it is a great place for tortillas, sandwiches and snacks.

## CATALAN

### Bilbao

C/Perill 33; tel: 93 458 9624; Mon–Sat 1–4pm, 9–11pm; €€; metro: Verdaguer or Diagonal; map p.134 C3

An animated atmosphere in this iconic Gràcia joint frequented by well-known journalists, artists and writers. It is especially busy at lunchtime and does a good-value menu of substantial dishes like roast chicken with *vino Rancio*, garlic and lemon and *trinxat* (a popular dish from the Cerdanya of fried potatoes and cabbage).

### Can Punyetes

C/Marià Cubí 189, tel: 93 200 9159; www.canpunyetes.com; daily noon–4pm, 8pm–midnight; €; FGC: Muntaner; map p.133 E4

Delicious grilled meats ranging from quail to rabbit to pigs' feet, over flaming coals, are the order of the day in this ancient two-storey dairy. Wash it all down with jugs of wine from the barrel and mourn the fact that places like these are are a dying breed.

### Casa Blava

Avda de Montserrat 26; tel: 93 674 9351; Tue–Thur 1–3.45pm, Fri–Sat 9–10.45pm, Sun 1–3.45pm; €; FCG: La Floresta

A pretty outdoor restaurant covered in a trailing vine where meat and even paella is cooked outdoors on an open wood fire. In January and February it does *calçots* (seasonal spring onions served with garlicky-nutty-peppery sauce). About 15 minutes' walk from the station, which is only a short ride from Plaça de Catalunya.

## FRENCH

### Artkuisine

C/Madrazo 137; tel: 93 202 3146; www.artkuisine.com; Mon 1.30–3.45pm, Tue–Sat 1.30–3.45pm, 7.30pm (for aperitifs) 9–11.45pm; €€€; metro: Gràcia; map p.133 E4

This newcomer to the city's fine-dining scene is run by a dynamic young French couple bursting with creativity. With its small but perfectly formed bar at the entrance, and more formal dining room at the back, it is worth getting dressed to dine here on expansive, ever-changing dishes such as braised oxtail with chocolate and banana and pickled partridge.

**Tipping:** As a general rule, if you're eating at the bar it's fine just to round up to the nearest euro. Otherwise a tip of 5–10 percent is considered the norm in restaurants.

113

# Shopping

Shopaholics rejoice. Barcelona is one of Europe's best-kept secrets when it comes to spreading the wealth. It may not have the reputation of London or Paris, but recent years have seen a number of seriously innovative projects open up, particularly in the world of fashion *(see Fashion, p.44–7)* and design. Being one of the most desirable places on earth for relocation means that Barcelona has an unprecedented mix of talent from overseas to add to its own stable of creative souls. For shops selling food, *see Food and Drink, p.57*, and for books *see Literature, p.77*.

## Shopping Malls

### Diagonal Mar
Avda Diagonal 3, Poblenou; tel: 93 567 7637; www.diagonal mar.com; Mon–Sat 10am–10pm; metro: El Maresme-Forum
One of the joys of going to Diagonal Mar is that you can get the tram from the Parc de la Ciutadella and go to the beach when you're done. Because it seems so far from the centre it offers a more relaxed shopping environment. Good on high-street labels and home ware; head to the swanky new Restaurante Klein (Rambla Prim 1; tel: 93 356 3088) in the Edifici Fòrum building for lunch.
SEE ALSO THE WATERFRONT AND POBLENOU, P.15

### L'Illa
Avda Diagonal 545–557, Eixample; tel: 93 444 0000; www.lilla.com; Mon–Sat 10am-9.30pm; metro: Maria Cristina; map p.133 C4
The definitive Barcelona shopping mall, nothing has topped it since it opened in the mid-1980s. Architecturally it's a dream – inspired by the Empire State Building lying on its side – while the shops are generous to a fault. Every major brand is here, mixed in with a little local talent. The food hall in the basement, meanwhile, is a cool place to do lunch – no, really – offering a wide selection of restaurants, from sushi and noodles to fruit bars.

## One-Stop Shops

### El Corte Inglés
Plaça Catalunya 14, Eixample; tel: 93 306 3800; www.elcorte ingles.com; Mon–Sat 10am–10pm; metro: Catalunya; map p.138 B4
This is the only name in Spain worth knowing when it comes to department stores, and Barcelona has a couple dotted around town. You can pick up just about anything here, from an emergency pair of hair straighteners to a digital camera to a bottle of bubbly to take home.

### FNAC
El Triangle, Plaça Catalunya 4, Eixample; tel: 93 344 1800; www.fnac.es; Mon–Sat 10am–10pm; metro: Catalunya; map p.138 B4

**Right:** Barcelona's malls house all the high-street favourites.

**Left:** shopping on Passeig de Gràcia in the Eixample.

### Art Escudellers

C/Escudellers 23–25, Barri Gòtic; tel: 93 412 6801; www.escudellers-art.com; daily 11am–11pm; metro: Drassanes; map p.138 B3

A vast space filled with pottery, glassware and souvenirs ranging from tacky to triumphantly kitsch. More practically, it's good for basic terracotta dishes and casseroles.

### Lladró

Passeig de Gràcia 11, Eixample; tel: 93 270 1253; www.lladro.com; Mon–Sat 10am–8.30pm; metro: Catalunya; map p.134 B1

Long considered a somewhat fusty, maiden-aunt style of pottery, a recent revamp of the brand has left Lladró looking uncannily cool. Its unmistakable pure white style still shines through, but now you can eschew the little shepherd girl in favour of one of hotshot Jaime Hayon's contemporary pieces instead.

## Interior Design and Household Items

### Coses de Casa

Plaça Sant Josep Oriol 5, Barri Gòtic; tel: 93 302 7328; www.cosesdecasa.com; Tue–Sat 10am–1.30pm, 5–8pm; metro: Liceu or Jaume I; map p.138 B3

For lovers of chintz, this is the Mediterranean version. Specialising in *Telas de Lenguas*, a typical textile style of Mallorca, they also offer custom-made patchwork quilts, tablecloths and cooking aprons; it will add a little sunshine to the home hearth.

### Ganiveteria Roca

Plaça del Pi 3, Barri Gòtic; tel: 93 302 1241; www.ganiveteria roca.es; Mon–Fri 9.45am–1.30pm, 4.15–8pm, Sat 10am–2pm, 5–8pm; metro: Liceu;

Though the service can be shoddy when it comes to getting any kind of advice for bigger purchases, this is nevertheless a good pit-stop for international magazines and newspapers, English-language books, CDs, DVDs and all manner of electronic goodies from digital cameras to MacBooks.

## Ceramics and Crafts

### L'Arca de l'Àvia

C/Banys Nous 20, Barri Gòtic; tel: 93 302 1598; www.larca delavia.com; Mon–Fri 10am–2pm, 5–8pm, Sat 11am–2pm; metro: Liceu; map p.138 B3

This charming little store stocks lace petticoats and doilies, costume jewellery and fans for ladies of a frivolous disposition. They also provided many of the costumes for *Titanic* and other period movies.

### Arlequí Mascares

C/Princesa 7, Born; tel: 93 268 2752; www.arlequimask.com; Mon–Sat 10am–8.30pm, Sun 10.30am–4.30pm; metro: Jaume I; map p.138 B3

A well-worn stop on the tourist route, this impressive mask shop stocks everything from sequinned Venetian eye patches to rather more sinister leather faces. Should you be in the market for such a thing, this is the place for you.

If you just want to have fun, walking is the way to go. The **Born** is full of quirky boutiques and concept shops that mix art and hairdressing, retro home ware and antiques. Small and compact, you could easily loose a day here combined with stopping for coffee or cocktails along the way. The **Barri Gòtic** is generally more mainstream, although there are still a few rare gems for those prepared to seek, combined with a little sightseeing and simply soaking up the atmosphere of the Old Quarter. The **Raval** is eclectic and arty, with lots of home-grown ideas to keep you amused. The **Eixample** is one big sprawl, so you'll want to don your trainers if you're going for this option. But it rewards by being crowd-free and strong on malls if you like to contain your addiction under one roof.

map p.138 B3

One of the oldest specialist knife shops in town, the range of blades here is mind-boggling, stocking over 9,000 brands. You can get anything here from a full set of Global's to a decorative shaving kit.

**Ivo & Co**

C/Rec 20, Born; tel: 93 268 3331; Mon–Sat 11am–3pm, 5–9pm; metro: Jaume I or Arc de Trimof; map p.138 C3

Think French farmhouse meets Cath Kidston and you get an idea of what's doing at Ivo & Co. Keep an open mind. It's great for hooks, glassware, dinner plates and kitchen utensils, wildly over-priced for books telling you how to seek treasure at jumble sales.

(Also at: boutique Plaça Comercial 3, tel: 93 268 8631)

**Papers Pintats Aribau**

C/Aribau 71, Eixample; tel: 93 453 2258; Mon–Fri 9.30am–1.30pm, 4.30–8pm; metro: Universitat; map p.134 A2

Trawl through the city's designer bars and you'll notice a recurring theme: one wall boasting loud, colourful, eye-catching wallpaper. If you feel you can't live without something similar in your own home, this specialist wallpaper shop sources all over the world, including the flamboyant designs of Tres Tintas BCN.

**RECD18**

C/Espaseria 7, La Ribera; tel: 93 268 0257; Mon–Thur 11am–2.30pm, 5–8.30pm, Fri–Sat 11.30am–2.30pm,

5–9pm; metro: Arc de Triomf or Jaume I; map p.138 C2

Good for smaller designer objects such as vases, crockery, lamps and other curios like cuckoo clocks, as well as bigger pieces of furniture. Perfect for jazzing up your desk or for an upmarket quirky gift.

**Última Parada**

C/Taulat 93 with C/Àvila 12, Poblenou; tel: 93 221 8078; www.ultimaparada.com; Tue–Sat 10am–1.30pm, 5–8pm; metro: Poblenou

Design junkies should not miss this Aladdin's cave of classic design. Vintage furniture, animal skin rugs, Verner Panton lamps, paintings and plump leather chairs and

**Right:** Papirum's artist-studio inspired displays.

**Left:** Vinçon's imaginative interior design.

sofas form just part of this extraordinary collection.

## Vinçon
Passeig de Gràcia 96, Eixample; tel: 93 215 6050; www.vincon.com; Mon–Sat 10am–8.30pm; metro: Diagonal; map p.134 B3

Barcelona's first design store remains one of the best, and it's a joy for window-shopping. Among the many desirable items for which Vinçon is known, ranging from moleskin notepads to bicycles, the latest crockery and cutlery collection by Ferran Adrià must surely make it onto the lists of the culinary high and mighty.

## Gifts

### Cereria Subirá
Baixada Llibreteria 7, Barri Gòtic; tel: 93 315 2606; Mon–Sat 9am–1.30pm, 4–7.30pm; metro: Jaume I; map p.138 B3

From religious to decorative, candles are a speciality of Barcelona. This is one of the oldest shops in Barcelona, dating from 1762.

### Fantastik
C/Mercè 31, Barri Gòtic; tel: 93 295 4877; www.fantastik.es; Mon–Sat 11am–9pm; metro: Drassanes; map p.138 B2

If you're deadly serious about spending money, then hop aboard the **Tomb-Bus**, which leaves at regular intervals from Plaça de Catalunya and transports happy shoppers (and their bags) along the Passeig de Gràcia and Diagonal. This is where you'll find the flagship stores and be able to do the most damage to your bank account.

The quirky range of gifts and trinkets at this colourful shop are not necessarily representative of Barcelona but fun none the less. Check out sombre-looking kitchenware from eastern Germany, South African soft toys and Day of the Dead paraphernalia from Mexico.

### Papelicola
C/Ferlandina 32, Raval; tel: 93 304 2666; Mon–Fri 4–8pm; metro: Sant Antoni; map p.137 E4

A modern take on the above, this is another little shop with bags of style. Bookbinders Hélène and Sandrina hand-make gorgeous fabric-covered notepads, artist's sketch pads and made-to-order items such as menu cards and travel journals.

### Papirum
C/Baixada Llibreteria 2; tel: 93 310 5242; www.papirum-bcn.com; Mon–Fri

10am–8.30pm, Sat 10am–2pm, 5–8.30pm; metro: Jaume I; map p.138 B3

Pint-sized and delightfully old-fashioned, the notepads and pens will bring out the inner Dickens in any aspiring writer. Indeed, the great and the good of Barcelona's literary set all stock up on their writerly craft here.

### WaWas
C/Carders 14, Born; no phone; Tue–Sat 10am–1.30pm, 5–8pm; metro: Arc de Triomf or Jaume I; map p.138 C3

If nothing but a kitsch memento of a lost weekend will do, then WaWas's Barcelona-themed stock should fit the bill. Think chocolate wrapped up in images of the *barrios*, paella postcards, and bags emblazoned with city icons.

# Sport

Catalans, while not remotely obsessed with the body beautiful, are an active lot in their spare time, and the council works hard to provide them with the sporting facilities they need. The legacy of the Olympic Games has also provided the city with some first-class venues for both spectator and participatory sports. On a more casual level, Barcelona's geography makes for spectacular routes for running or cycling, such as the seafront, Montjuïc or the Carretera de les Aigües on the fringes of the Collserola hills. *See also Walks and Tours, p.128,* for details of bicycle tours in the city.

## Basketball

Basketball is hugely popular in Catalonia, which has produced some of the world's finest players (notably, on the current scene, Pau Gasols). The Barça basketball team is part of the football club, and matches are played in the **Palau Blaugrana** (tel: 93 496 3600), next to Nou Camp.

## Bowling

**Namco Station**
Diagonal Mar Centre, Poblenou; tel: 93 356 2500; www.namco.es; Sun–Thur noon–midnight, Fri–Sat noon–3am; admission charge; metro: El Maresme Fòrum

A bowling alley, which also has pool tables, inside the Diagonal Mar shopping centre *(see p.114)*.

**Pedralbes Bowling**
Avda Doctor Marañón 11, Les Corts; tel: 93 333 0352; www.bowlingpedralbes.com; Sun–Thur 10am–2am, Fri–Sat 10am–4am; admission charge; metro: Collblanc/Zona Universitaria
Fourteen bowling lanes, snooker and table football.

## Cycling

A map of cycle lanes is available in tourist offices.
**Barcelona by Bicycle**
C/Esparteria 3, Born; tel: 93 268 2105; www.biketoursbarcelona.

com; Mon–Fri noon–4pm; metro: Barceloneta/Jaume I; map p.138 C2
Bicycles and skates for hire, or accompanied cycling tours of the Old Town.
**Biciclot**
Passeig Marítim 33, Barceloneta; tel: 93 221 9778; www.bikingin barcelona.com; summer: Mon–Thur 10am–3pm, 4–8pm, Fri–Sun 10am–3pm, 4–9pm, winter: Fri–Sun 10am–3pm, 4–6pm; metro: Barceloneta; map p.139 D1
Bikes for hire, smack on the beach.

## Football

Football is close to a religion in Barcelona. When the favourite local team, **Barça**, is playing, you will know all about it: from the traffic jams to the explosion of fireworks, car horns and bugles following a victory.
**Nou Camp**
Avda Arístides Maillol, Les Corts; tel: 93 496 3600; www.fcbarcelona.com; Mon–Sat 10am–6.30pm, Sun 10am–2pm; admission charge; metro: Collblanc or Maria Cristina; map p.132 A4
One of the largest stadiums in the world. Its museum is one

**Left:** FC Barça fans gear up for a match.

ming: June–Aug Mon–Fri 10am–4pm, Sun 10am–7pm; metro: Penitents

This urban 'hard' park has a large outdoor pool/lake, complete with Eduardo Chillida sculpture. Boats can be hired in the winter. Ideal for small children.

**Piscines Bernat Picornell**
Avda de l'Estadi 30–40, Montjuïc; tel: 93 423 4041; www.picornell.com; June–Sept: Mon–Sat 9am–9pm, Sun 9am–8pm, Oct–May: Mon–Sat 10am–7pm, Sun 10am–4pm; metro: Espanya; map p.136 B3

Olympic pool in a beautiful location on Montjuïc.

## Tennis

**Tennis Municipal de Montjuïc**
C/Foixarda 2–4, Montjuïc; tel: 93 325 1348; Mon–Fri 8am–10.30pm, Sat–Sun 8am–10pm; metro: Espanya; map p.136 A3

Reasonably priced council-run tennis courts.

## Water Sports

**Base Nautica de la Mar Bella**
Platja de Bogatell, Avda Litoral; tel: 93 221 0432; www.base nautica.org; metro: Poblenou

All types of boats for hire by qualified sailors, along with sailing courses for the inexperienced. Windsurf hire.

---

*Petanca* is the fiercely popular Catalan answer to *boules*, played on public courts dotted all over town. For details of these *see* www.bcn.cat (click on 'sport' and then 'facilities'), and for competitions *see* www.fcpetanca.org.

---

of Barcelona's most visited, and includes a tour of the grounds. Now there's a *nuevo* Nou Camp on the horizon, a Norman Foster project inspired by Gaudí's mosaics, that will cloak the building in the team's colours.

## Golf

There are many courses all over Catalonia (see full list on www.gencat.net/probert). To play, it is essential to prove membership of a recognised club. Weekend fees are usually double the weekday fee.

## Gyms

*See* the Club Natació under **Swimming**, *right*.

## Motor Racing

The Formula One racing track **Catalunya Circuit** is about

20km (12 miles) from Barcelona, in Montmeló (for information, tel: 93 571 9700).

## Skiing

During the season, cheap weekend excursions are available from Barcelona to the Pyrenean resorts, some of which can be reached by train (check out www.lamolina.com).

## Swimming

**Club Natació Atlètic-Barceloneta**
Plaça del Mar, Barcelona; tel: 93 221 0010; www.cnab.org; Mon–Fri 6.30am–11pm, Sat 7am–11pm, Sun 8am–8pm (5pm Oct–mid May); metro: Barceloneta; map p.138 B1

Large indoor pool overlooking the sea, and two outdoor pools. It has a well-equipped gym, sauna and jacuzzi.

**Parc de la Creueta del Coll**
C/Mare de Deu del Coll 87, Tibidabo; tel: 93 211 3599; www.parcsijardins.com; swim-

---

**Right:** muscled locals head to the waterfront for a workout.
**Left:** a poster advertises the 2007 Eurobasket tournament.

# Tapas Bars

In a city not traditionally known for its tapas, small plates are now the preferred way of eating. Each week something new opens, with many of the country's top chefs targeting Barcelona for new tapas projects ranging from traditional to transformational. Trends aside, there are still a handful of places that haven't changed for decades, and more often than not it's in these hidden gems that you'll find the true spirit of the *barrio*. The art of the *tapeo* (to hop from bar to bar) is a convivial affair in which partakers go from bar to bar for a drink and a snack in each. *See also Bars and Cafés, p.28–35 and Restaurants, p.104–13.*

## Barri Gòtic

### Cala del Vermut
C/Copons 2; tel: 93 317 9623; €; Mon–Fri 10am–5pm, 6.30–11pm, Sat–Sun noon–4.30pm; metro: Urquinaona; map p.138 B3
This tiny but delightful bar on two floors has duck-egg blue walls lined with barrels of artisan vermouth. Do as locals do and enjoy yours over ice and a slice of orange, with a plate of salty anchovies and slices of sweet and spicy chorizo.

### Irati
C/Cardenal Casañas 17; tel: 902 520 522; daily noon–midnight; €; metro: Liceu; map p.138 B3
One of the first of a bevy of Basque bars that opened in the 1990s. Grab what you fancy from the great variety of *pintxos* (snacks on a toothpick) arranged along the bar tops, but don't overfill: the best are the hot *pintxos* that emerge at regular intervals from the kitchen.

### Kiosko Universal
La Boqueria stall number 691; tel: 93 317 8286; Tue–Sat 8am–4pm; €; metro: Liceu; map p.138 A3
Few Barcelona food experiences beat sitting amid the highly charged atmosphere of the Boqueria food market (*see p.78*). There's plenty to

**Left:** experience tapas in style at Taller de Tapas.

Catalan wines are available by the glass, along with tasty platters of local cheeses and charcuterie.

### Euskal Etxea
Placeta Montcada 1–3; tel: 93 310 2185; €; Mon 7pm–midnight, Tue–Sat noon–4pm, 7pm–midnight; metro: Jaume I; map p.138 C3

Housed in the Basque cultural centre, this is arguably the best place in town to sample San Sebastián-style tapas. Toppings range widely from spider crab in hot sauce to smoked Idiazábal cheese with quince paste, while the *txacolín* – Basque white wine with a slight fizz – flows freely.

## The Waterfront and Poblenou

### Arola
Hotel Arts, C/Marina 19–21; tel: 93 483 8090; www.arola-arts.com; €€€; Wed–Sun 1.30–4.30pm, 8.30–11pm; metro: Ciutadella-Port Olímpic; map p.139 D2

This smart, sexy, surf-inspired bar at the Arts *(see p.68)* is the project of Sergi Arola, who has two stars for his restaurant La Broche in Madrid. Popular with Spanish celebs, it's the place to come if you like to see and be seen. Expect posh, expensive tapas such

---

| Prices for an average meal with wine: |
| --- |
| **€** under €25 |
| **€€** €25–€40 |
| **€€€** €40–€60 |
| **€€€€** over €60 |

choose from when it comes to eats, but the Kiosko Universal comes out tops for fresh fish and seafood caught from neighbouring stalls, and it's a fraction of the price of the city's swankier seafood restaurants. A heaped platter of grilled squid, mussels, *navajas* (razor clams), clams and other treats from the deep with nothing more than a drizzle of olive oil and lemon, washed down with lashings of cool, crisp white wine, makes a feast fit for a king. Arrive before 1.30pm to avoid queuing.

### El Portalón
C/Banys Nous 20; tel: 93 302 1187; Mon–Sat 9am–midnight; €; metro: Jaume I; map p.138 B3

Barrels, pitchers of wine, nicotine-stained walls and

**Left:** Kiosko's chefs in action.
**Right:** fresh *pintxos*.

old men playing dominoes – this place oozes atmosphere, and the set menu chalked on a blackboard is excellent value. Don't miss their *potajes* (bean or chick pea stews) in winter.

## Sant Pere and Born

### El Bitxo
C/Verdaguer I Callis 9; tel: 93 268 1708; €; Mon–Thur, Sun 1–4pm, 7pm–midnight, Fri–Sat 1–4pm, 7pm–1am; metro: Urquinaona; map p.138 B4

This pint-sized bar is handily located across the road from the Palau de la Música, but don't make that your only reason to visit. Good-quality

as deconstructed *patatas bravas* and *fetge-gras* soup – oh, and a fabulous terrace for chilling out beneath the stars.

### La Bombeta
C/Maquinista 3; tel: 93 319 9445; €; Tue–Mon 10am–midnight; metro: Barceloneta; map p.138 C1

At the other end of the scale, La Bombeta is cheap, cheerful and usually rammed. It's a classic neighbourhood bar famed for its *bombetas* (mashed potato balls stuffed with meat and topped with chilli sauce and alioli), but it's also good for sardines, grilled squid and jugs of lethal sangria.

## Montjuïc, Poble Sec and Sant Antoni

### Bar Seco
Passeig de Montjuïc 74; tel: 93 329 6374; €; Tue–Sun 11am–11pm; metro: Poble Sec; map p.137 D2

Small and cosy with a chilled-out vibe, this relative newcomer is run by the younger fraternity of Barcelona's slow-food members. The emphasis here is on organic and local products such as small-production cheeses and sausages from free-range pigs, as well larger *raciones* like pasta with beetroot. There's also a good range of organic beers.

### El Funicular
C/Vallhonrat 28; tel: 93 325 8538; €€; Tue–Sat 1–4pm, 8.30–11pm; metro: Poble Sec; map p.137 C3

Virtually unknown outside Barcelona circles, El Funicular nevertheless is a much-loved, rough-around-the-edges *bar de barrio* tucked away in the upper reaches of Poble Sec. Spanking fresh seafood such as sweet, tiny *tallarines* (purple-lipped clams) as well as more fright-

---

#### C/Mercè
Before the Mediterranean became the Passeig Marítim, galleons would haul anchor here at the back of the Calle Mercè. Sailors first gave thanks for safe passage at the church and then indulged in wine, women and song along this emblematic street. Head for **La Plata** for the freshest tiny fried fish, **La Celta** for tender octopus on a wooden platter, **El Corral** for cider poured from above the head and *pan amb tomàquet* topped with gossamer-thin slices of *cecina* (cured beef), and finally, but only for the brave, pop into the bar with no name recognised by an abusive parrot outside, for a shot of *pacharán* (sloe-flavoured anis from Navarra) and *chistorra* (paprika-flavoured sausage) in a bun.

---

ening fare like cockscombs are the highlights.

### Inopia
C/Tamarit 104; tel: 93 424 5231; www.barinopia.com; €; Tue–Fri 7–11pm, Sat 1–3.30pm, 7–11pm; metro: Poble Sec; map p.137 D4

A phenomenon since the day it opened, Inopia is the brainchild of Albert Adria – the pastry chef at El Bulli, considered by many to be the finest restaurant in the world. Get there early if you want to snag a stool at the bar or the one high table, otherwise be prepared to wait for superlative ingredients-led tapas. Don't miss ventresca tuna with Raf tomatoes and sweet onions, home made *croquetas*, and the sardine *flauta* (finger-thick, chewy yet crisp baguette).

### Quimet y Quimet
C/Poeta Cabanyes 25; tel: 93 442 3142; €€; Mon–Fri noon–4pm, 7–10.30pm, Sat noon–4pm; metro: Paral·lel; map p.137 D3

Another Barcelona institution is now in the hands of a fourth generation of Quims, and the tapas is more inventive than ever. It's standing room only at this pocket-sized bar stacked with wine bottles (each week features a

**Right:** Taller de Tapas.

**Left:** most markets have bars serving freshly prepared tapas.

different cava, white and red by the glass) that marry perfectly with treats like cream cheese, king prawns and truffle honey; caper pâté, smoked mussels and balsamic syrup; and rustic country pâté with confit chestnuts.

## The Eixample
### Bodega Sepúlveda
C/Sepulveda 173; tel: 93 454 7094; €€; Mon–Sat 9.30am–1am, Sat 12.30–4pm, 7.30pm–1am; metro: Universitat; map p.137 E4
This old-school tapas bar and restaurant is perfect for discovering Catalan delicacies such as stuffed squid, baby broad beans with blood sausage, *escalivada* and hearty *cassola* stews of clams in wine and garlic. Perfect after catching a movie at nearby Floridablanca cinema *(see p.53)*, it serves food until midnight.
### Cata 181
C/Valencia 181; tel: 93 323 6818; www.cata181.com; €€; Mon–Sat 6pm–1am; metro: Provença; map p.134 A2
New-wave, creative tapas at Cata 181 provide a fresh perspective on the classics. The bright white interior flirting with the odd streak of orange

---

Prices for an average meal with wine:
€ under €25
€€ €25–€40
€€€ €40–€60
€€€€ over €60

---

is a fitting background to vivacious tapas such as pigs' trotters with figs and honey, truffle omelettes and buckets of foam.
### Taller de Tapas
Rambla Catalunya 49–51; tel: 93 487 4842; www.tallerde tapas.com; €€; Mon–Sat 7.30am–1am, Sun noon–1am; metro: Passeig de Gràcia; map p.134 B2
Big, bustling and brimming with good things, the latest opening of the Taller group, like its sister restaurants, is all about high-quality products, freshly made on the spot. Located in a smart, Modernista block on the leafy Rambla Catalunya with high ceilings and oak floors, plus a leafy terrace, means you can do tapas in style with all the comforts of a proper restaurant. Don't miss sausages with *fetge*, local Blanes prawns, crisp artichoke shavings and Nuri's soft goat's cheese drizzled with honey.
Also at: Plaça Sant Josep Oriol 9, Barri Gòtic; tel: 93 301 8020

---

and C/Argenteria 51, Born; tel: 93 268 8559.

## Upper Neighbourhoods
### Fragments Cafè
Plaça de la Concòrdia 12, Les Corts; tel: 93 419 9613; www.fragmentscafè.com; €€; Wed–Thur, Sun 12.30pm–midnight; Fri, Sat 12.30pm–2am; metro: Les Corts; map p.132 C4
A newcomer from the same person that bought you Tapioles 53 *(see p.111)*, this deli-style tapas bar occupies a corner of a lovely plaça in Les Corts. Enjoy hunks of smoked salmon, tiny red peppers stuffed with goat's cheese and top wines by the glass at the bar. There's a dining room and garden out back for burgers, pasta and stronger drinks.
### Oli en un Llum
C/Bon Pastor 6 bis; tel: 93 210 7397; www.luzdegas.com; €€; Mon–Thur, Sun 7.30pm–2am; Fri–Sat 7.30pm–3am; FCG: Gràcia; map p.133 E3
A classy little place to have up your sleeve if you get peckish late, this is popular with the uptown crowd. The designer cocktail bar specialises in stout mixed with lager (better than it sounds) while a sultry, sexy dining room downstairs is cool for making your moves over the best *jamón Ibérico* and fried-egg sandwiches on earth.

# Theatre and Dance

**M**uch of the theatre in Barcelona is in Catalan or Spanish. This poses less of a problem when dealing with modern dance or ballet at the Liceu *(see below)*, and Barcelona is OK on both counts. Make no mistake, the Catalan capital does not come close to London or New York when it comes to treading the boards, but you can still have fun at some of the musicals like *Cabaret* on theatre mile at the Teatre Condal *(see box)*. If you want to singalong though, bear in mind the lyrics have been translated from the original.

## Theatres

### Gran Teatre del Liceu
La Rambla 51–59; tel: 93 485 9913; www.liceubarcelona.com; Mon–Fri 11am–2pm, 3pm–8pm (general information), Mon–Fri 2pm–8pm, Sat–Sun 1 hr before performance (box office); metro: Liceu; map p.138 A3
Although better-known as an opera house, the Liceu also puts on dance performances.
SEE ALSO MUSIC, P.92

### Teatre Lliure
Plaça Margarida Xirgú, Montjuïc; tel: 93 289 2770;

For the latest hit musicals try **Teatre Condal**, Avda Paral·lel 91, Poble Sec; tel: 93 442 3132; www.teatral.net/condal; metro: Poble Sec; map p.137 D3

www.teatrelliure.com; Mon–Fri 11am–3pm, 4.30–8pm, Sat–Sun 2 hrs before show (box office); metro: Poble Sec; map p.136 C3
In the theatre complex on Montjuïc you will find a cluster of stages, although it is rare to find anything in Eng-

lish. The one exception is the Lliure, which, in a forward-thinking move, subtitles into English on Wednesdays. The performances themselves tend towards heavy adaptations of the classics, particularly Shakespeare. Great for serious aficionados, perhaps a little too earnest for the casual theatregoer.

### Teatre Nacional de Catalunya
Plaça de les Arts 1, Eixample; tel: 93 306 5700; www.tnc.es;

**Left and below:** a flamenco dancer at Los Tarantos.

**Who's who:** Barcelona's most revolutionary playwright was **Frederic Soler Pitarra**, who scribed his works in an upstairs room of an old clock shop at C/Avinyó 56 in the Barrí Gòtic. It is now a good traditional bistro named Pitarra (tel: 93 301 1647; Mon–Sat 1–4pm, 8.30–11pm; metro: Jaume I; map p.138 B2). Fast forward to the 21st century and the name to watch is **Calixto Bieito**, notorious for his risqué productions.

box office: Wed–Fri 3–8pm; Sat 3–9.30pm, Sun 3–6 pm (special times during morning events); metro: Glòries; map p.1355 E1
Designed by Ricardo Bofill, this state-of-the-art theatre hosts mainly highbrow Catalan and Spanish productions. Pre-booking is available up to one hour before the start of the performance.

**Teatre de la Riereta**
C/Reina Amalia 3, Raval; tel: 93 442 9844; www.lariereta.es; hours: variable; metro: Sant Antoni; map p.137 E3
For a more down-to-earth experience, this cute little theatre has two or three English-language productions a year, often amateur but occasionally good fringe. The quality fluctuates, but their willingness to experiment is admirable and if you are a fan of mime, modern dance and alternative performance art it is well worth keeping an eye on the schedule.

**The Giggling Guiri**
C/ Riereta 7, Raval; tel: 93 329 9009; www.gigglingguiri.com; hours: variable; metro: Sant Antoni; map p.137 E3
Housed in a fabulously kitsch and intimate theatre with cabare-style décor (book a table if you can), the line-up of British and American comedians here is impressive. Many of the acts are award-winners like Paul Sinha – a gay Asian GP turned comedian – and the loveable Josie Long. Dates rotate between here and Madrid.

### Dance Venues

**Los Tarantos**
Plaça Reial 17, Barri Gòtic; tel: 93 319 1789; www.masimas.com; daily 8.30pm, 9.30pm, 10.30pm; metro: Liceu; map p.138 B3
If you are looking for authentic flamenco you are in the wrong city. The real stuff is down south in the bars of Granada, Seville and Jerez. If you just want a little foot-stamping and twirly dresses this is the one of the better centrally located venues in town.

**Tinta Roja**
C/Creu dels Molers 17, Poble Sec; tel: 93 443 3243; www. tintaroja.net; Wed–Thur 8am–2am, Fri–Sat 8am–3am, Sun 7pm–1am; metro: Poble Sec; map p.137 D3
For fans of the *milonga* this off-the-beaten-path bar-cum-theatre is a true gem. From the pretty wooden bar to the swinging trapeze you know you've stumbled on somewhere special. Tango classes take place every Wednesday at 9–10.30pm with Argentinian ace Carmen Cubero, and there are random live performances through the month.

**Left:** the Teatre Nacional de Catalunya.

# Transport

Getting to Barcelona from most parts of Europe is easy and relatively inexpensive, and trains are now offering a viable alternative to flying. Once there, you will find the city an eminently walkable one, but for sights outside the centre, buses and the metro system are both efficient and affordable. For awkward journeys or at night, taxis are plentiful and reasonably priced. If you are going to be travelling much outside Barcelona, it is a good idea to hire a car, but it will be more of a disadvantage than an asset in the city itself, where traffic is heavy and parking can be a problem.

## Arrival

### BY AIR

Barcelona Airport is 12km (7 miles) south of the city in El Prat, and easily reached by train, bus or taxi. There are three terminals: A and B for international flights; C is for domestic flights. (Airport tel: 902 404 704.)

**Trains** to Sants, Passeig de Gràcia and Estació de França depart from the airport every 30 minutes and cost €1.30 each way. **Aerobús**, an efficient bus service, is normally the best way to and from the airport, however. It runs to Plaça de Catalunya from each terminal every 12 minutes, stopping at strategic points en route. It operates until midnight or so, and the fare is €4.05 single and €7 return.

A **nightbus**, the N17, runs from Plaça de Catalunya/ Ronda Universitat from 11pm to 5am.

To reach most central parts of Barcelona by **taxi** will cost about €20 plus an airport supplement and a token amount for each suitcase.

### BY RAIL

A more eco-friendly (if expensive) option from other parts of Europe is to take the **Trenhotel** which runs daily from Paris to Estació de França in Barcelona, and several days a week from Zurich, Geneva and Milan. The **Talgo** runs twice daily between Montpellier and Barcelona, to either Sants or Estació de França. Montpellier connects with the **TGV**, the French high-speed train.

For international train information and reservations, tel: 902 243 402. For national train information, tel: 902 240 202, www.renfe.es. A helpful website is www.seat61.com.

### BY BUS

Several UK bus companies operate a service to Barcelona, the largest of which is **Eurolines** (tel: 902 405 040; www.eurolines.es). In the UK, contact **National Express** (tel: 08705 808 080; www.nationalexpress.com).

## Transport within Barcelona

**Tickets** work interchangeably on the metro, buses, trams and FGC trains within the city. A flat-rate single

Anyone in Barcelona for any length of time might consider the excellent, Ajuntament-supported bike scheme, **Bicing**. There are stands all over the city where card-holders can pick up a bike, use of which is free for the first 30 minutes, and only 30¢ per half-hour thereafter (up to a maximum of 2 hours). For more information, *see* www.bicing.com.

**Right:** Barcelona's public transport system is easy to navigate.

**Left:** there are Bicing stands all over Barcelona.

lying towns such as Sant Cugat, Terrassa, Sabadell, Manresa and Igualada. It is a useful service for reaching the upper parts of Barcelona and for parts of Tibidabo and the Parc de Collserola.

The metro ticket is valid on this line within Zone 1, but travel beyond is more expensive. Within the town the timetable is the same as the metro, but beyond it varies according to the line. (Check in a station or call 010 for information. FGC, tel: 93 205 15 15.)

### CYCLING
Barcelona is now a cyclist-friendly city, with cycle lanes, parking facilities and many great traffic-free places to cycle, such as the port, marinas, and along the beach front from Barceloneta to Diagonal Mar.
SEE ALSO WALKS AND TOURS, P.128

### TAXIS
All Barcelona taxis are black and yellow, and show a green light when available for hire. Rates are standard and calculated by meter, starting at a set rate and clocking up at a rate governed by the time of day: night-times, weekends and fiestas are more expensive.

ticket costs €1.30 (or a 10-journey ticket, which can be shared, costs €7.20) and can include up to four changes within 1 hr 15 mins. Tickets are available on buses (single journey only) and at stations, banks, tobacconists and tram stops.

### METRO
Trains are frequent and cheap, but few metro stations have lifts, so those in wheelchairs or with pushchairs may find buses easier. Trains run 5am–midnight Mon–Thur and Sun, 5am–2am Fri and all night Sat.

### BUS
The bus service is good for reaching the areas the metro doesn't, and for seeing more of Barcelona. Most buses run from 5 or 6am until 10pm. There are some night services (the Nit bus), but lines vary, so check on the map or at bus stops.

### FGC
The local train service, Ferrocarrils de la Generalitat de Catalunya (FGC), interconnects with the metro, looks like the metro and functions in the same way, but extends beyond the inner city to out-

# Walks and Tours

If the thought of going on a 'tour' sends shivers down your spine – and not in a good way – take comfort in the fact that Barcelona now offers a wide range of personalised and alternative ways of seeing the city that are worth the extra expense. For first-time visitors, tour buses are a smart, time-efficient way of getting orientated, and if you prefer to go at your own pace there are a plethora of bicycle and scooter rental outlets to choose from. Listed below is a selection of some of the best ways of getting to know the city. This is the Barcelona you never dreamed of.

## By Bike

### Fat Tire Bike Tours

C/Escudellers 48, Barri Gòtic; tel: 93 301 3612; www.fattire biketours.com; enquire for times; tour €€€; metro: Dras-sanes or Jaume I; map p.138 B3

These distinctive chunky-tired bikes have become almost as much a symbol of the city as yellow cabs in New York. It is hard to stroll around without seeing a group of them meandering towards you. Part of their appeal is they are big, slow and comfort-able, meaning that you have time to sit back and enjoy the view. Several tours leave each day during the summer, and it is worth having an experienced guide along, but you can go it alone. Rides take you through the Barri Gòtic, past many of the major sights and along the beach, capped off with a beer.

## By Boat

### Catamaran Orsom

Moll de Drassanes (at the bot-tom of the Ramblas at Plaça Colon); tel: 93 441 0537; www.barcelona.orsom.com; enquire for prices and times; metro: Drassanes; map p.138 A2
Take to the high seas with this classy catamaran and see another side of Barcelona. Trips include sunset cruises around the harbour with live jazz sessions, day and half-day cruises, as well as per-sonalised trips to Sitges (see p.22) and the Costa Brava (catering provided).

## By Bus

### Barcelona Tours

Tel: 93 261 5679; www.barcelonatours.es; depart 9–9.30am at Plaça de Catalunya, end 6.20–8.45pm; one-day pass €21, two-day pass €25; metro: Catalunya; map p.138 B4
The orange bus tour may not be as frequent as the compe-tition (the *bus turístic*), but the route is longer and more comprehensive. The deal is

**Getting away from it all:** The Collserola parkland is a vast swathe of hills and pine forest. You could easily spend a day hiking around up here, pic-nicking in secluded spots with fabulous views, or stopping in at one of several mountain *merenderos* (shacks) serving hearty grilled meats and flagons of wine.

**Right:** the view from the Collserola mountain range.

**Left and below left:** the fun and informative Fat Tire Bike Tours are a great way to see the city.

**Night hiker:** Every Tuesday evening between 8.30pm and 9pm Marc Ros (tel: 617 956 572; marc@desconnecta.com) takes a group of adventurers up into the Collserola mountain range just behind the city. Kitted out with a pair of Nordic walking poles and a head torch you set off across the ridge, pines silhouetted against a night sky and the twinkling lights of the city far below. Walks last about one and a half hours and are often followed by wine and tapas. From €18. Daytime Nordic hikes are also available around Barceloneta and Montjuïc.

the same: you can jump on and off at will. An obvious place to start and end is outside the Hard Rock Café on Plaça de Catalunya. Just sit back and enjoy.

## By Foot
### Follow the Baldie
No phone; http://oreneta.com/baldie/; enquire for walk dates and prices

Not for the faint of heart, but these wonderfully eccentric walks offered by Trevor Ap-Simon are a real tonic after the endless generic guff on offer. Expect to see Barcelona as you have never seen it before: take the highs with the lows on the **Old Quarter tour**, which points out bag snatchers' haunts as well as Roman ruins; **Posh Barcelona** gives an insight into how the Catalan bourgeoisie spend their money; while the **last farmer of Horta** points out the unlikely survival of city farms on the edge of the metropolis. If you are thirsting for more, Trevor also takes excursions out of town through wine country, factory land and on a creepy kooky **Night of the Tarantula**.

### Cook & Taste
La Rambla 58, 3rd floor; tel: 93 302 1320; www.cookandtaste.net; enquire for times and prices; metro: Liceu or Catalunya; map p.138 A3

This isn't strictly a tour, but the informative shopping trip to the market will cast light on all those unmentionables, and there is a certain joy in knowing you are going to eat it afterwards. The most popular classes are for the simple pleasures: gazpacho, tortilla, paella and crema catalana washed down with country wine from the Penedès. More advanced sessions are also available.

# Atlas

The following streetplan of
Barcelona makes it easy to find the
attractions listed in our A–Z section.
A selective index to streets and sights
will help you find other locations
throughout the city

## Map Legend

| | | | |
|---|---|---|---|
| Autopista | | ⟨M⟩ | Metro Station |
| Dual carriageway | | | Ferrocarrils de la Generalitat de Catalunya (FGC) |
| Main road | | 🚐 | Bus station |
| Minor road | | ✈ | Airport |
| Footpath | | 🚡 | Cable car |
| Railway | | | Funicular railway |
| Pedestrian area | | ℹ | Tourist information |
| Notable building | | ★ | Sight of interest |
| Park | | ⚲ | Beach |
| Hotel | | ⛪ | Cathedral / church |
| Urban area | | ☾ | Mosque |
| Non urban area | | ✡ | Synagogue |
| Cemetery | | ⚊ | Statue / monument |
| | | ✚ | Hospital |

| | | | |
|---|---|---|---|
| p132 | p133 | p134 | p135 |
| p136 | p137 | p138 | p139 |

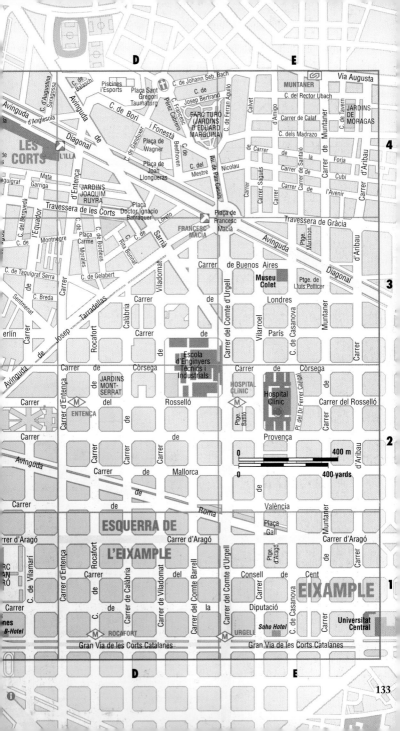

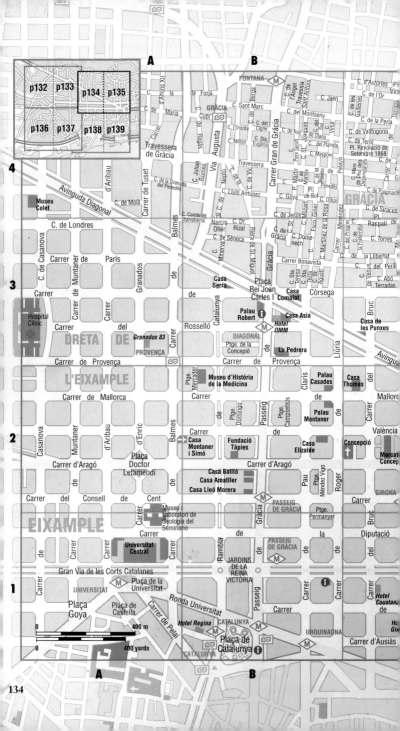

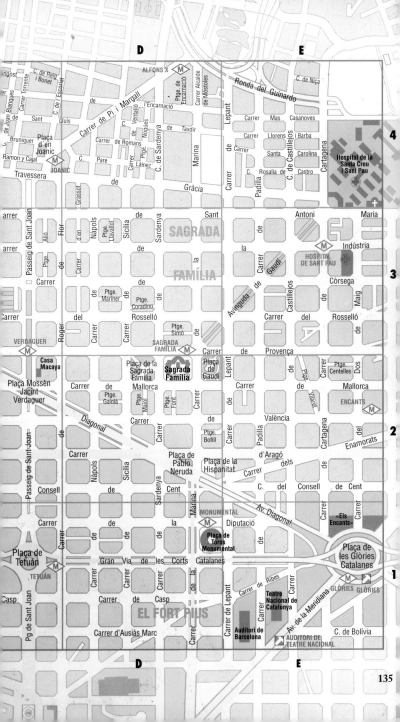

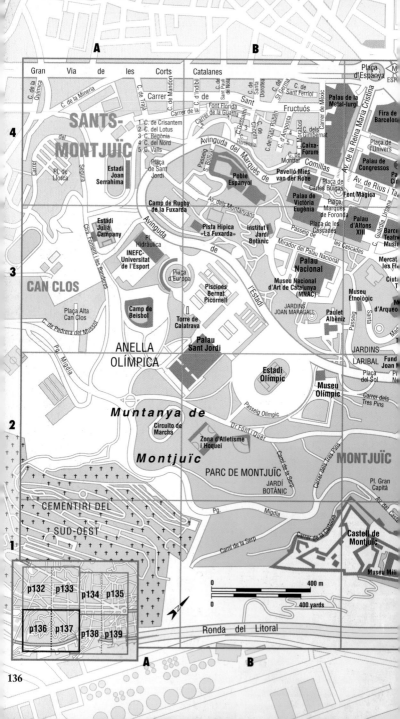

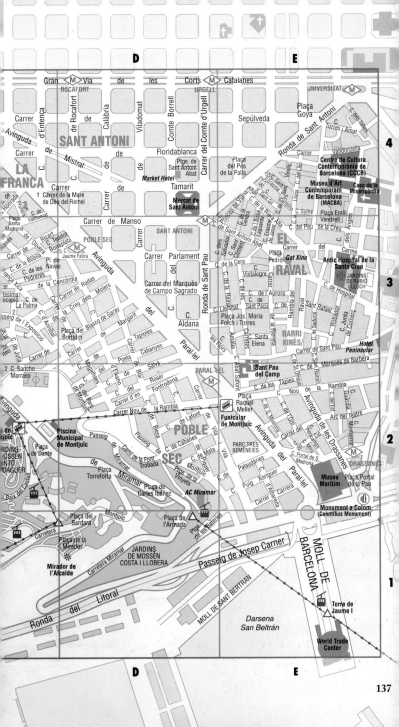

A

B

Carrer    de    Casp

**4**

Ronda de Sant Antoni
Carrer de Pelai
Mesón de Castilla
Hotel Ciutat Vella
Plaça de Catalunya
Ronda
URQUINAONA
C. del Bruc
Carr
C. del Tigre
Valldonzela
C. de Sant Antoni
C. Elisabets
Centre de Cultura Contemporània de Barcelona (CCCB)
Museu d'Art Contemporani de Barcelona (MACBA)
CATALUNYA
CATALUNYA
C. Fontanella
de
Sant
C. Vicenç
C. Paloma
C. de Ferlandina
C. Sant Gil
Parr. Major de Sta Anna
Pere
C. de la Riera Alta
Casa de la Misericòrdia
C. de Santa Anna
Carrer Comtal
Via
Laietana
C. d'Ortigosa
Palau de la Música Catalana
Plaça Àngels
Casa Camper
Pintor Fortuny
C. de la Canuda
Montsió
Carrer de Sant Pere Més
Pensió 2000
EL
RAVAL
Plaça Emili Vendrell
C. del Peu de la Creu
Rivoli Ramblas
Hotel 1898
Av. Portal de l'Àngel
Sant Pere Mit
C. Sant Pere Més Ba
Carrer del
Betlem
Palau Moja
Sant Pere
Plaça Pedró
Gat Xino
Antic Hospital de la Santa Creu
Carme
Portaferrissa
CASC AN
Riera Baixa
C. Hospital
JARDINS DE RUBIÓ I LLUCH
Pl. Gardunya
Palau de la Virreina
Mercat la Boqueria (Sant Josep)
BARRI
Sant Felip Neri
Plaça Antoni Maura
Av. Catedral
Museu Diocesà
Av. F. Cambó
Mercat Santa Caterina
CASC AN
LA-RIBE
**3**
C. de Sant Rafael
C. de Sant Vicenç
C. de Junta de Comerç
Santa Maria del Pi
GÒTIC
Museu del Calçat
Catedral
Museu Frederic Marès
Santa Àgata
Plaça Santa Caterina
Cordes
Hotel Ci
Rambla del Raval
Sant Agustí
LICEU
Palau de la Generalitat
Casa dels Canonges
Museu d'Història de la Ciutat
Plaça Salvador Seguí
Gran Teatre del Liceu
C. de la Boqueria
Carrer Ferran
Carrer Jaume I
JAUME I
C.de la Prince
Hotel Peninsular
Hotel Espanya
Plaça Reial
Plaça Sant Miquel
Museu Tèxtil i de la Indumentària
Museu Picasso
Sant Pau del Camp
C. Nou de la Rambla
Palau Güell
Casa de la Ciutat Ajuntament
Església dels Sants Just i Pasteur
Museu Barbier-Mueller d'Art Precolombí
Marquès de Barbera
C. des Escudellers
G. Orwell
Santa Maria del Mar
Arc del Teatre
Plaça del Teatre
Parròquia Sant Sperit
Laietana
Correus
Hotel Park
C. de Còdols
DRASSANES
Centre d'Art Santa Mònica
Via
La Llotja
Av. Marqu de l'Argen
Av. del Paral·lel
Portal de Santa Madrona
Museu de la Cera
La Mare de Déu de la Mercè
Delgació del Govern
Escola de Nàutica
Carrer Ample
Carrer de la Mercè
Duquesa de Cardona
Passeig d'Isabel II
BARCELO
Plaça Portal de la Pau
Bonic B&B
Passeig de Colom
M
Museu Marítim
Monument a Colom (Columbus Monument)
MOLL DE LA FUSTA
Museu d'Història de Catalunya
Plaça Pau Vila
**2**
MOLL DE LES DRASSANES
Port Autònom/ Junta d'Obres
MOLL D'ESPANYA
Marina Port Vell
BARCELONET
Golondrinas (Boat Trips)
Rambla de Mar
C.la Ma
Pg. Joan de Borbó
MOLL DE BARCELONA
PORT VELL
Plaça Barceloneta
Mercat Barceloneta
Plaça Poeta Bo
IMAX
L'Aquàrium
Maremàgnum
C. Baluard
C. Almirall Cervera
Torre de Jaume I
**1**
0      400 m
0      400 yards
World Trade Center
Hotel 54
C. del Varadero
Sea Point Hotel
Torre de St Sebastià
Plaça Palmeres
Acuario
Platja Sant Seba

A

B

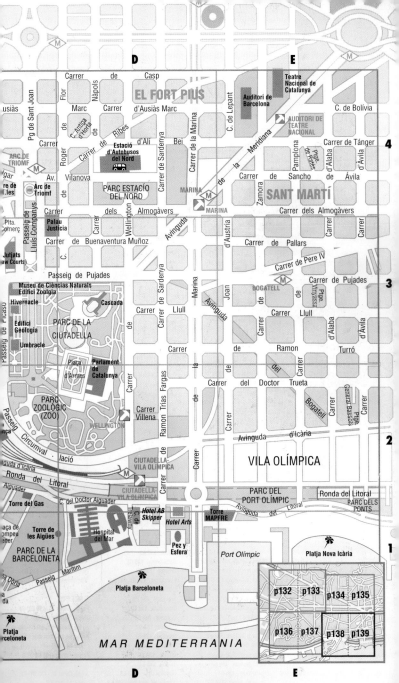

Carrer de Casp
Carrer de Napols
Flor
Carrer de Sant Joan
Marc
Carrer d'Ausiàs Marc

**EL FORT PIUS**

**Auditori de Barcelona**

Teatre Nacional de Catalunya

C. de Bolívia

**AUDITORI DE TEATRE NACIONAL**

Carrer d'Alí
Carrer de la Marina
C. de Lepant
Meridiana
de la

**ARC DE TRIOMF**

Roger de Carrer de Ribes
Av. Vilanova
**Estació d'Autobusos del Nord**
Carrer de Sardenya
Bei

Carrer de Tánger

Pamplona
Carrer d'Alaba
Carrer d'Àvila

**4**

**Arc de Triomf**

**PARC ESTACIÓ DEL NORD**

MARINA

Carrer de Sancho de Ávila

Zamora

**SANT MARTÍ**

Passeig de Lluís Companys
Carrer dels Almogàvers
Wellington
Avinguda d'Àustria
**Palau Justícia**

Carrer dels Almogàvers

Carrer de Buenaventura Muñoz
Carrer de Pallars

**Plta. Comerç**
**Jutjats (Law Courts)**

Carrer de Pere IV

Passeig de Pujades
Carrer de Sardenya
Carrer de Pujades

**Museu de Ciències Naturals Edifici Zoologia**
**BOGATELL**
Pge. Vinyassa

**Hivernacle**
Llull
Marina
Joan
Carrer Llull
d'Alaba
d'Àvila

**Cascada**
**PARC DE LA CIUTADELLA**
Avinguda

**3**

**Edifici Geologia**

**Umbracle**
Carrer
Ramon
Turró

Plaça d'Armes
**Parlament de Catalunya**
la
Carrer del Doctor Trueta
Bogatell

**PARC ZOOLÒGIC (ZOO)**
Carrer Villena
**WELLINGTON**
Ramon Trias Fargas
Carrer
de
Avinguda d'Icària

**2**

Passeig Circumval·lació
lació
de
**CIUTADELLA VILA OLÍMPICA**
**VILA OLÍMPICA**

gda d'Icària
**Ronda del Litoral**
Aiguader
**CIUTADELLA VILA OLÍMPICA**
**PARC DEL PORT OLÍMPIC**
Ronda del Litoral
**PARC DELS PONTS**

**Torre del Gas**
C. del Doctor Aiguader
**Hotel AB Skipper**
**Torre MAPFRE**

aça de Pompeu
**Torre de les Aigües**
**Hotel Arts**
Avinguda del Litoral

**PARC DE LA BARCELONETA**
**Hospital del Mar**
**Pez y Esfera**
**Port Olímpic**
**Platja Nova Icària**

**1**

Passeig Marítim

**Platja Barceloneta**

Porta
da

**Platja celoneta**

**MAR MEDITERRÀNIA**

| p132 | p133 | p134 | p135 |
| p136 | p137 | p138 | p139 |

**D**                    **E**

## Selective Index for Street Atlas

### PLACES OF INTEREST

140

# Index

Insight Smart Guide: Barcelona
Written by: Sally Davies, Tara Stevens, Katie Addleman, Gavin Boyd
Edited by: Joanna Potts
Proofread and indexed by: Neil Titman
Photography: All pictures © APA/Greg Gladman and Gregory Wrona except:
Alamy 67B, 118–119; Art Archive 61TR; Bridgeman Art Library 61BL; Corbis 49BL; Hemis 66B; Istockphoto 48–49, 94–95, Press Association 63TR; Topfoto 62R, 63BR
Cover picture by: Alamy; bottom: Getty
Picture Manager: Steven Lawrence
Maps: James Macdonald; Neal Jordan-Caws
Series Editor: Jason Mitchell

First Edition 2008
© 2008 Apa Publications GmbH & Co.

Verlag KG Singapore Branch, Singapore.
Printed in Singapore by Insight Print Services (Pte) Ltd
Worldwide distribution enquiries:
Apa Publications GmbH & Co. Verlag KG (Singapore Branch) 38 Joo Koon Road, Singapore 628990;
tel: (65) 6865 1600;
fax: (65) 6861 6438
Distributed in the UK and Ireland by:
GeoCenter International Ltd
Meridian House, Churchill Way West, Basingstoke, Hampshire RG21 6YR;
tel: (44 1256) 817 987;
fax: (44 1256) 817 988
Distributed in the United States by:
Langenscheidt Publishers, Inc.
36–36 33rd Street 4th Floor, Long Island City, New York 11106; tel: (1 718) 784 0055; fax: (1 718) 784 0640l